The Legal System of Scotland

Fourth edition

Derek Manson-Smith

July 2008

Fòcas Luchd-Caitheimh   Consumer Focus

TSO
ation & publishing solutions

The information contained in the publication is believed to be correct at time of manufacture. Whilst care has been taken to ensure that the information is accurate, the publisher can accept no responsibility for any errors or omissions or for changes to the details given.

A CIP catalogue record for this book is available from the British Library.

A Library of Congress CIP catalogue record has been applied for.

First published 1997
Second Edition 2001
Third Edition 2004
Fourth Edition 2008
ISBN 978 011 497347 6

Contents

Acknowledgements

I am grateful to Sarah O'Neill, Legal Officer at the Scottish Consumer Council, for her editorial guidance on the 4ᵗʰ edition of this book.

I would also like to thank staff in the Scottish Government Justice and Communities Directorate General, the Scottish Court Service, the Scottish Legal Aid Board, the Law Society of Scotland and the Faculty of Advocates for their comments on particular chapters.

I have tried to provide an accurate reflection of the legal system of Scotland as it stood at 30 June 2008.

Derek Manson-Smith

July 2008

About Consumer Focus Scotland

Consumer Focus Scotland started work in October 2008. Consumer Focus Scotland was formed through the merger of three organisations – the Scottish Consumer Council, energywatch Scotland, and Postwatch Scotland.

Consumer Focus Scotland works to secure a fair deal for consumers in both private markets and public services, by promoting fairer markets, greater value for money, and improved customer service. While producers of goods and services are usually well-organised and articulate when protecting their own interests, individual consumers very often are not. The people whose interests we represent are consumers of all kinds: they may be patients, tenants, parents, solicitors' clients, public transport users, or shoppers in a supermarket.

We have a commitment to work on behalf of vulnerable consumers, particularly in the energy and post sectors, and a duty to work on issues of sustainable development.

www.consumerfocus-scotland.org.uk

Origins and sources of Scots law

1.1 Introduction

Following the Union of 1707, the laws and legal institutions of Scotland and of England and Wales were not merged but remained separate. Similarly, the laws and legal institutions of Ireland were not merged after the Union between Great Britain and Ireland of 1801. While the law of Northern Ireland is closely modelled on English law, which applies in England and Wales, Scots law is markedly different. It has its own originality, determined by its distinctive history and its relationship with other legal systems.

This was confirmed by the Scotland Act 1998, which in 1999 devolved certain powers from the United Kingdom Parliament to a Scottish Parliament. The Scottish Parliament can pass legislation on devolved matters without going through the United Kingdom Parliament in Westminster. The Acts of Union remain on the statute book and the Scotland Act ensures that the Acts of Union are construed in the light of the Scotland Act.

1.2 Types of legal systems

Legal systems are often distinguished from each other according to whether they are civilian law systems or common law systems.

Civilian law systems are those that are historically derived from Roman law. Most European countries adhere to civilian law systems.

Common law systems, however, are those derived from English law, and the countries that have common law systems are England and Wales and Northern Ireland, most Commonwealth countries, and most of North America.

Historically, the essential difference between the two systems is that in civilian systems the rules of law are derived from first principles as expounded by the authoritative writings of jurists, while in common law systems the rules are derived from the decisions of judges in specific cases.

Scots law has its origins in the European civilian law systems, but has gradually developed similarities to the English common law approach, particularly the acceptance of judge-made law, or precedent, as a source of law.

1.3 Brief history of the development of Scots law

From the 11th century, Scotland was a feudal kingdom, which involved the granting of land in return for services, such as produce from the land or military service, and the courts were presided over by local landowners. While the monarch was in theory responsible for dispensing 'secular justice', that is, criminal and non-criminal or civil justice, the task was actually delegated to local 'sheriffs'. The church courts applied canon law in various matters including family matters and the inheritance of moveable property.

In the absence of universities in Scotland until the 15th century, and later of universities giving adequate training in law, Scots lawyers were educated in Europe, particularly in France, Germany, Flanders and the Netherlands, where Roman law was taught.

The structure of the judiciary began to take shape in 1532, when the Lords of Council and Session were permanently reorganised as a College of Justice with a wide civil (that is, non-criminal) jurisdiction. Jurisdiction is the right or authority to apply laws and administer justice; and the district or area over which this authority extends. The 15 judges of 'the Session' became Senators of the College of Justice who sat together in one court.

In the 16th century the Faculty of Advocates and the Writers to the Signet evolved and were given the exclusive right to plead in court (as advocates) and to act as solicitors.

There continued to be three main differences between Scots and English law:

1) In the English common law courts between the 12th and the 19th centuries, court cases had to be started by using particular forms of action, so that each type of claim had its own name, and had to be raised in a particular way. Court action was not possible unless one of these forms of action was used, so there could not be a right without a legal remedy. In Scotland, the earlier forms of action, known as brieves and similar to the English writ, gave way to a more flexible procedural form (called a 'summons') which could be adapted to fit any number of different types of claim. As long as there was a right there were few procedural barriers to obtaining a remedy, as long as the action had been raised in the right court.

2) Scots law recognised the distinction between the strict letter of the law on the one hand, and the equitable discretion of judges to soften the rigours of the law on the other. But it did not follow the English practice of setting up equity (a right as founded on the laws of nature; moral justice) as a separate system, with its own rules and procedures and courts.

3) In England, juries were used in all civil cases to decide the facts. This was not so in Scotland.

In the late 17th century, Lord Stair, Lord President of the Court of Session, and the first of the so-called 'institutional writers', published his *Institutes of the Law of Scotland*. In this, Stair set out the whole of Scots law as a rational, comprehensive, coherent and practical set of rules deduced from common-sense principles. Where possible, Stair gleaned his law from reported Scottish decisions and statutes, or he was guided by Roman law, canon law or the Romano-Germanic systems.

Stair was followed in later centuries by other institutional writers such as Erskine, Bell and Hume, whose restatements of the law incorporated new law that had been developed by judges' decisions or enacted in statutes.

In 1707, the United Kingdom of Great Britain was created as a result of the Union of the Parliaments of Scotland and England.

Gradually, English law began to replace Roman law as the main external source of Scots law. Scots students were less likely to study law in Europe and the practice stopped with the Napoleonic wars. The House of Lords became the final court of appeal for Scots civil cases, and the English doctrine of judicial precedent, or subsequent cases being bound by decisions in earlier relevant cases, came to be more strictly applied.

The reform of the Court of Session in the early 19th century contributed to the move towards English legal methods. Two Inner House Divisions were created to hear appeals from Outer House judges and these appeal decisions were followed by Outer House judges in later cases. Despite the fact that judges in the House of Lords were likely to be English lawyers, judges in Scotland began to follow the decisions of the House of Lords. As Scotland's industrial, commercial and cultural experience began to grow more like that of England, it became obvious that English law was a more relevant source of law than Roman law. The influence of English law continued to grow, so that now, although a House of Lords decision on appeal from an English court is not binding on Scottish courts, it is nevertheless usually regarded as persuasive if the case concerns principles that apply in both legal systems. Scottish and English courts are not bound by each other's decisions but they do consider them persuasive, especially if they interpret United Kingdom statutes.

The civil (that is, non-criminal) law in Scotland rests on more generalised rights and duties than in England. Scots law still traditionally argues deductively from principles despite the influences of English law. Also, there continue to be many differences in the substantive law, that is the actual law concerned with rights and duties, to be contrasted with the legal process, that is court procedure.

The present judicial system is substantially the same as it was following the Union of Parliaments in 1707. The Court of Session has almost universal civil jurisdiction, which means that almost any non-criminal case with a value of £5,000 or more can be raised in the Court of Session as an alternative to the local sheriff court. The Court of Criminal Appeal, which hears appeals from decisions of the High Court of Justiciary as well as lower courts, was not set up until 1926. The local sheriff courts, presided over by full-time, legally-qualified judges, became the main local courts dealing with the bulk of civil and criminal cases. The burgh courts or justices of the peace courts continued to deal with minor criminal offences. These were replaced by district courts in 1975, following reorganisation of local government, and continued to perform the same function after further local government reorganisation in 1996.

In March 2008, a programme of court unification began by replacing district courts with justice of the peace courts under the administration of the Scottish Court Service. The programme is due for completion in October 2009. At the time of writing, the provision of civil justice by the courts in Scotland, including their structure, jurisdiction, procedures and working methods, was under review.

1.4   The Parliaments

1.4.1 Introduction

Before 1707, Scotland was an independent state with its own Parliament with an important law-making function. Although some Acts of the original Scottish Parliament remain in force, most have been repealed or can be regarded as no longer in force because of disuse.

1.4.2 The United Kingdom Parliament

In 1707, both English and Scottish Parliaments technically ceased to exist, and the United Kingdom Parliament with English, Scottish and Welsh members and peers, was constituted as a new legal institution, sitting in the same premises as the former English Parliament in Westminster.

Under the doctrine of sovereignty of Parliament, Acts of the United Kingdom Parliament were and continue to be absolutely binding on all courts, taking precedence over all other sources of law including the common law, except European Union law. Also, any Act of the United Kingdom Parliament can repeal or amend statutes whether passed by the United Kingdom Parliament, the former Scottish or English Parliaments or the current Scottish Parliament. The courts cannot challenge the United Kingdom Parliament's power of repeal or amendment, except to the extent such an act is inconsistent with European Union law.

1.4.3 The Scottish Parliament

Pressure for constitutional change from the late 1960s led to a demand for a Scottish Parliament with law-making powers, which was approved by a referendum in 1997. Following the referendum, the United Kingdom Parliament passed the Scotland Act 1998, which devolved powers from the United Kingdom Parliament to Scotland, for which the Scottish Parliament was created in Edinburgh in May 1999.

The devolution settlement provided the Scottish Parliament in Edinburgh with devolved powers within the United Kingdom. The Scotland Act specifies the powers reserved to the United Kingdom Parliament. Those that are not reserved are devolved to the Scottish Parliament.

Devolved powers on matters such as education, health and local government, which used to be dealt with by the parliament in Westminster, are now decided by the Scottish Parliament. Reserved powers on matters with a United Kingdom or international aspect, such as social security, defence and foreign affairs, are reserved and decided by the United Kingdom Parliament.

The Scottish Parliament operates as a self-contained and fully-functioning parliament in its own right. It can pass legislation on devolved matters without going through the United Kingdom Parliament, and it has powers to alter the rate of tax. While the United Kingdom Parliament retains the right to legislate on any matter, the convention of devolution is that the United

Kingdom Parliament will not normally legislate on devolved matters without the consent of the Scottish Parliament.

The Scotland Act provides for the United Kingdom or Scottish Law Officers to challenge Bills and Acts of the Scottish Parliament in the courts (see Chapter 12).

1.5   The Scottish Government

The Scotland Act also provides for a devolved administration in Scotland, which is referred to in the Act as the Scottish Executive. Following the change in the administration in May 2007, the Scottish Executive became known as the Scottish Government and is referred to as such throughout this publication. The Scottish Government is responsible for all devolved matters. At devolution, the powers and duties exercised by United Kingdom Ministers in Scotland relating to devolved matters were transferred to the Scottish Ministers, the collective term for members of the Scottish Government. Most of the responsibilities previously held by the Scottish Office became part of the remit of the Scottish Government. The Scottish Government also formulates policy and when it decides that primary legislation is required it brings draft Bills to the Scottish Parliament.

1.6   The European Union

1.6.1 Introduction

European Union derives from a set of international treaties concluded among a number of European counties since the 1950s. The principal treaties are the Treaty of Paris of 1951, which set up the European Coal and Steel Community, the Euratom Treaty of 1957, which created the European Atomic Energy Community, and the Treaty of Rome of 1957, which founded the European Economic Community. The Communities created by these treaties are legal persons distinct from their member states in international and domestic law, with their own independent rights, powers and duties. The treaties also provided for the creation of a parliamentary assembly, an inter-governmental council, an independent commission and a supervisory court.

The United Kingdom became a member of the European Communities on 1 January 1973, following the European Communities Act 1972 which gave effect to Community law in the United Kingdom and enabled the government to make regulations and orders implementing the country's obligations as a member of the Communities.

The European Communities evolved by way of other treaties, such as the Single European Act 1986, to form the European Community, and the Treaty on European Union 1992 (the Maastricht Treaty), which seeks a fuller European union by means of various institutional changes to the Community itself. In recognition of the importance of this development, the European Community became known as the European Union.

Further developments were the Treaty of Amsterdam 1997, which concerns the Union's foreign policy and the free movement of its citizens, and the Treaty of Nice 2000, which provided for the enlargement of the European Union, with ten countries of central and eastern Europe, the Mediterranean and the Baltic joining in 2004, and two more countries joining in 2007. The latest phase of evolution is the Treaty of Lisbon 2007, which amends the existing treaties in order to ensure that the new European Union of 27 member states can work effectively.

The European Union is a supra-national organisation, although it is not a federation like the United States of America. It makes laws through directives, regulations and decisions that have to be adopted by the national law of each member state (see 1.8). These apply to a large and increasing number of fields, ranging from consumer law to employment protection to intellectual property to immigration to company law.

1.6.2 The European Commission

The European Commission, which is based in Brussels, initiates and implements Union policy and legislates under its own powers and under those delegated by the Council of Ministers (see 1.6.3). The commissioners, who are nominated by their governments, owe their allegiance to the Union, not to their governments. A civil service of directorates-general supports the commissioners.

1.6.3 The Council of Ministers of the European Union

The Council of Ministers represents member states, coordinates their views and must approve most Union legislation. One minister from each member state's government sits on the Council, although at any one time different ministers may represent their government, depending on the subject in question.

As meetings of the Council are infrequent and the representative ministers are limited to the subject under discussion (for example, social issues, agricultural issues), the main work of the Council is carried out by the Committee of Permanent Representatives (known as COREPER, after the French abbreviation). COREPER is made up of national civil servants of the member states. It deals with all business that goes before the Council, and if its views are unanimous the Council accepts its decision.

1.6.4 The European Parliament

The European Parliament represents the electorate of member states and its members are directly elected. Formerly a largely supervisory, consultative and deliberative body, the parliament has acquired greater influence and power through a series of treaties, particularly the Treaty of Maastricht 1992 and the Treaty of Amsterdam 1997 (see 1.6.1). It is now a legislative parliament, exercising powers similar to those of national parliaments.

Membership of the European Parliament is allotted in different proportions to each member state. The parliament sits for one week a month in Strasbourg, where the European Parliament has it seat. Committees based in Brussels do most of its work, and it has a secretariat based in Luxembourg.

1.6.5 The European Court of Justice

The European Court of Justice, which sits in Luxembourg, ensures that Union law is correctly interpreted and observed by member states. Attached to it is the Court of First Instance, which was introduced to reduce the delays in cases coming before the Court of Justice. Some cases can be appealed from the Court of First Instance to the European Court of Justice.

The courts deal with several types of cases. They decide 'direct actions' where they hear the whole proceedings – these include actions against Union institutions. They also decide 'enforcement actions' brought by Union institutions against member states that are alleged to have failed to carry out their obligations under various treaties. Of more importance to the legal system of Scotland, the Court of Justice hears preliminary references from national courts and tribunals. Any national court or tribunal hearing a case that involves the interpretation or validity of Union law may, if it wishes, send that part of the case to the court for an authoritative ruling, which binds the national court. National courts have to apply European Union law – if there is any doubt, the issue can be referred to the Court of Justice. The national court decides questions of fact and gives the final decision (see 5.1).

1.7   The European Convention on Human Rights

The European Convention for the Protection of Human Rights and Fundamental Freedoms, usually known as the European Convention on Human Rights (ECHR), is a treaty signed by most western European counties, including the United Kingdom. The treaty was drawn up by the Council of Europe, a treaty organisation set up by European states to promote human rights.

The ECHR requires its signatories not to permit infringements of:

* A right to life

* Freedom from torture or inhuman or degrading treatment

* A right to liberty and security

* A right to family life

* A right to peaceful enjoyment of possessions

* A right to education

- A right to free elections

- A right to freedom of movement and residence

- The right of entry to a state of which one is a national and a right not to be expelled from it.

The European Commission on Human Rights is made up of a nominee of each signatory to the Convention. The Committee of Ministers of the Council of Europe is made up of the foreign ministers of countries that are members of the Council of Europe. The European Court of Human Rights has one judge from each signatory state.

1.7.1 The Human Rights Act 1998

While the European Convention on Human Rights has always been part of United Kingdom law, the Human Rights Act 1998 directly incorporates provisions from the convention into United Kingdom law, so that the convention rights are enforceable in the United Kingdom courts. Formerly a case could be taken to the European Court of Human Rights only when domestic remedies had been exhausted.

The Human Rights Act makes it unlawful for a public authority to act incompatibly with convention rights, and allows for proceedings against the authority to be brought in an appropriate court or tribunal if it does so. Judicial review (see Chapter 12) provides a remedy in such circumstances.

The Act also requires all legislation to be interpreted and given effect as far as possible compatibly with convention rights. From its inception, the Scottish Parliament would be outwith its legislative competence if it passed a Scottish Bill that conflicted with the ECHR. Scottish judges can declare primary legislation incompatible with the convention. In such circumstances, a minister may amend the legislation to bring it into line with convention rights, or quash or disapply subordinate legislation (see Chapter 12).

The Scotland Act provides for dealing with the consequences of Acts of the Scottish Parliament or actions of the Scottish

Government that are found to be outwith their powers in relation to convention rights. The courts have powers to limit the retrospective effects of such Acts or actions. Provision is also made for the United Kingdom Parliament to make subordinate legislation to remedy the defect.

There are different procedures for dealing with Acts of the United Kingdom Parliament and actions of the United Kingdom government in these circumstances.

Scottish courts and tribunals must take account of the case law of the European Court of Human Rights, the European Commission on Human Rights and the Committee of Ministers of the Council of Europe. They are also bound to develop the common law compatibly with convention rights.

1.8 Sources of Scots law

The main sources of Scots law are judge-made law, certain legal writings having 'Institutional' authority (see 1.3) and, most importantly, legislation. The first two sources are sometimes referred to as the common law of Scotland. Legislation is formally-created law, comprising the law created by or under the authority of the United Kingdom and Scottish Parliaments, and by the European Union (see 1.6.1).

United Kingdom legislation consists of statutes (Acts of Parliament) made by the United Kingdom Parliament in Westminster on reserved matters and subordinate legislation authorised by the United Kingdom Parliament.

Scottish legislation consists of Acts made by the Scottish Parliament on devolved matters (see 1.4.3), and subordinate legislation authorised by the parliament. Subordinate legislation in Scotland falls into two main groups:

Regulations and rules made by Scottish Ministers or directorates of the Scottish Government. These are known as statutory instruments, which are published and are subject to a degree of parliamentary scrutiny and control, and they normally apply throughout Scotland. For example, the Housing (Scotland) Act

2006 was introduced to address problems of condition and quality in private sector housing; the Housing (Scotland) Act 2006 (Prescribed Documents) Regulations 2008, which were made under that Act prescribe the documents that a seller or selling agent must possess and provide in response to a request from potential buyers from 1 December 2008.

Byelaws made by local authorities (which apply only in their areas) and other public authorities (which apply only within the sphere of their functions), under powers delegated to them by the Scottish Parliament. For example, local authorities have made byelaws under the Local Government (Scotland) Act 1973 that make it an offence for anyone to drink in public in a designated place.

European Union legislation consists of primary legislation found in the treaties that established the framework and authority of the European Communities, and secondary legislation made by the co-decision of the European Parliament, the Council of Ministers and the European Commission. Secondary legislation includes:

Regulations, which have the force of law without the need for confirmation by the national legislatures of member states.

Directives, which are binding as to the result to be achieved but have to be implemented by member states in whatever way they feel appropriate.

Decisions, which can be addressed to member states, corporations or individuals. They are binding but affect only those to whom they are addressed.

1.9 Further reading

Bradley, A W & Ewing, K D, *Constitutional and Administrative Law*. Pearson Education Ltd, Harlow, 2007. £35.99.

Cuthbert, Mike, *Nutshells European Law*. Sweet and Maxwell, London, 2006. £8.

Finch, Valerie & Ashton, Christina, *Human Rights and Scots Law*. W Green, Edinburgh, 2002. £42.

Lesguillions, Henry, *Public Law*. W. Green, Edinburgh, 2007. £34.

Munro, Jane, *Constitutional Lawbasics*. W. Green, Edinburgh, 2005. £12.50.

O'Rourke, Stephen Robb-Russell, *Glossary of Legal Terms*, 4th edition. W Green, Edinburgh, 2004. £12.50.

Branches of Scots law

2.1 Introduction

The two most important branches of the law are civil and criminal law. Civil law is about deciding disputes between two parties – individuals or administrative authorities or commercial organisations. Criminal law is where the state prosecutes alleged criminal activity. Private prosecutions in the criminal courts are possible, although rare.

2.2 Civil law

The civil law can be separated into two parts – public law and private law.

2.2.1 Public law

Public law regulates and controls the exercise of political and administrative power within the state. It concerns the activities of the United Kingdom and Scottish Parliaments, the courts, Scottish Ministers (the collective term for members of the Scottish Government, the devolved administration in Scotland), local government, and public bodies, for example, the regulators of privatised utilities, such as those for energy and telecommunications, and their relationships with private individuals.

In their relationships with private individuals, public bodies are within the competence of the Scottish Parliament except when they deal only with reserved matters (see 1.4.3) or have been designated as 'cross-border public authorities'. Cross-border public authorities are those that deal with matters both within and outwith the legislative competence of the Scottish

Parliament. They are within the competence of United Kingdom government ministers.

The Scotland Act 1998 provides for dealing with the consequences of Acts of the Scottish Parliament or actions of the Scottish Government that are found to be outwith their powers (see 1.4.3 and 1.7.1).

Public law provides mechanisms to challenge the decisions made by such bodies, such as judicial review (see Chapter 12) and tribunals (see Chapter 7).

2.2.2 Private law

Private law deals with the rights and obligations of citizens among themselves. The major areas of private law are:

Family law, which includes marriage, divorce, civil partnership, dissolution of a civil partnership, residence, contact and guardianship of children, and adoption.

The law of contract, which includes the sale of goods, consumer credit, insurance, and partnership.

The law of delict, which deals mainly with civil wrongs for which the wrongdoer must pay compensation, such as defamation, damage to property or personal injury caused by negligence.

The law of property, which concerns the right to enjoy property and the obligations arising from that enjoyment, ownership or possession of land or moveable property, the creation and administration of trusts, and succession (the division of someone's property following his or her death).

Other areas of private law include:

- Mercantile law, which deals with the law regulating trade, companies and bankruptcy.

- International private law, which regulates the jurisdiction of the Scottish courts in cases where people or property from outwith Scotland are involved. It determines whether Scots law or foreign law (in the sense of a legal system distinct from Scots law, including English law and Northern Irish law) is applicable to a legal question. It also provides for the recognition and enforcement of foreign judgments in Scottish courts.

2.3 Criminal law

The criminal law is not concerned with relationships between individuals or organisations, but rather with the maintenance of the peace and order of the community, and the prosecution and punishment of crime.

Generally, ignorance of the law is no defence. Therefore, in criminal matters, statute (that is Acts of the United Kingdom or Scottish Parliaments) or the common law should define crimes as clearly as possible, so that people have a fair notice of the restriction on their liberty of action.

In most cases, the prosecution has to prove that the person accused of the crime intended to do what he or she is accused of doing or failing to do.

More serious crimes are tried by a judge and jury on 'indictment'; others are tried by a judge without a jury (see 8.1).

Sometimes crimes are categorised by the kind of interest infringed – such as, offences against property (for example, theft), non-sexual injury (for example, assault), sexual offences (for example, rape), offences against the state (for example, treason), against public order and welfare (for example, breach of the peace), and against the course of justice (for example, perjury).

2.4 Further reading

Ashton, C, Chalmers, J, Craig, V, Finch, V, Grier, N, Shiels, R, *Understanding Scots Law*. W Green, Edinburgh, 2007. £29.

3

The judicial system

The judicial system is made up of all the agencies that exist to resolve disputes, disagreements over claims and legal rights, and conflicts of interest, and to apply the law.

The main characteristic of the system is the existence of separate courts and tribunals for civil, criminal and administrative matters. Another characteristic is the division of the courts into inferior and superior courts. Inferior courts have jurisdiction locally, while superior courts have jurisdiction over the whole of Scotland. The sheriff court and the district and justice of the peace courts are known as inferior courts. The Court of Session, the High Court of Justiciary and the House of Lords are known as superior courts. A further characteristic is the division of courts and tribunals into those that have original jurisdiction, also known as courts or tribunals of first instance, which hear cases for the first time, and those of appellate jurisdiction, which hear appeals from other courts or tribunals. Some courts perform both functions at different times.

Litigation, or court action, in Scotland is generally an adversarial or contentious procedure, rather than an inquisitorial or investigative procedure, as is found in many other legal systems. This means that the judge usually does not act as an inquisitor and make an investigation but presides over a contest between two parties, ensuring that the rules of law are applied and followed, and decides the case on the basis of the legal arguments and the facts submitted.

In civil proceedings, it is for the person with a claim (the pursuer) to decide who to pursue (the defender), on what grounds of law, what facts to present, and who to call as witnesses. The defender can also present evidence and call witnesses. In criminal proceedings, it is for the Crown (the prosecutor) to decide who to prosecute (the accused), on what grounds of law, what evidence to produce, and who to call as witnesses. The accused person can similarly present evidence and call witnesses. The prosecutor may drop a charge at any stage and the judge cannot pass sentence on any finding of guilt unless asked to do so.

The two sides have to convince the jury, if there is one. The judge simply answers any questions on matters of fact or law, explains the law to the jury, and puts its verdict into effect.

The civil courts

4.1 The sheriff court

The sheriff court deals with the bulk of civil litigation in Scotland. It is a local court, presided over by the sheriff who is a legally-qualified judge and exercises a very wide jurisdiction (see 10.1.2). There is a sheriff court in every city and most towns.

Sheriff courts are organised into six sheriffdoms. These are: Grampian, Highland and Islands; Tayside, Central and Fife; Lothian and Borders; Glasgow and Strathkelvin; North Strathclyde; and South Strathclyde, Dumfries and Galloway. Each sheriffdom (except Glasgow and Strathkelvin) is divided into sheriff court districts of which there are 49. For example, Tayside, Central and Fife is divided into the districts of Alloa, Arbroath, Cupar, Dundee, Dunfermline, Falkirk, Kirkcaldy and Stirling. There are currently 141 sheriffs in post, including 30 floating sheriffs, who are permanent, full-time sheriffs appointed to serve in any sheriffdom as required. Busier courts may have more than one sheriff; for example, Glasgow has 24, with four floating sheriffs available if required, and Edinburgh has 16, with one floating sheriff.

There may be up to 80 part-time sheriffs at any one time.

Each sheriffdom has a sheriff principal who is responsible for the speedy and efficient conduct of business, and each sheriff court has a sheriff clerk who runs it from day-to-day.

The sheriff hears cases when they are first raised (at first instance) in the sheriff court of a district. In common law, the sheriff is 'judge ordinary of the bounds', that is, the judge with jurisdiction in all cases arising in his or her sheriffdom that are not allocated to other courts. The sheriff court also deals with appeals from, or review of, many local authority and other administrative decisions, for example, licensing appeals. Juries are not used in civil cases in the sheriff court. Most types of case first heard by a sheriff can be appealed to the sheriff principal, or directly to the Court of Session.

Many different types of action can be brought before the sheriff court. In civil cases, the pursuer must normally bring his or her case in the sheriffdom of the defender's domicile, that is, where he or she normally lives or has a place of business; or the place where a contract was to be carried out; or where the incident occurred that resulted in the legal action. However, special rules apply to 'consumer contracts', which allow the consumer to bring his or her case in the sheriffdom of either his or her domicile or that of the defender, and to certain other types of action, such as those for damages.

The sheriff court currently has exclusive jurisdiction in actions for sums of £5,000 or less and in many statutory applications and appeals. The value of the subject matter that the court may deal with has, with very few exceptions, no upper limit, and a wide range of remedies may be granted. The sheriff court can consider actions for, among other things, debt, separation, divorce, damages, rent restriction, possession (for example, of a house), actions to make someone do something (for example, to deliver goods in fulfilment of a contract) and actions affecting the use of property, leases and tenancies, and actions to regulate the residence of or contact with children.

The sheriff court cannot deal with certain types of cases. For example, judicial review (see Chapter 12), and under the Companies Act 1985, a sheriff cannot hear petitions, that is written applications to the court, to wind up a company with a paid-up share capital of greater than £120,000. Certain actions, for example, some of those involving status (declarator of marriage, nullity of marriage), are reserved for the Court of Session. Other cases, such as those concerning employment matters, are not normally heard in the sheriff court because they have their own tribunal (see 7.3).

The Court of Session is the supreme civil court in Scotland. It is both a court of first instance and a court of appeal and sits only in Parliament House in Edinburgh. There is provision for 34 Court of Session judges. In addition, temporary judges may be appointed. One judge is seconded part-time as Chairman of the Scottish Law Commission (see 11.4). The Court of Session consists of two houses – the Outer House and the Inner House.

4.2.1 The Outer House

Twenty-four judges, called Lords Ordinary, form the Outer House. They are exclusively concerned with deciding cases for the first time, and sit alone, usually without a jury.

The Outer House's jurisdiction is wide and includes all kinds of civil claims unless the law expressly excludes them. It covers actions on commercial cases, contract, reparation, property and personal status, petitions for the appointment of judicial factors and curators, that is, people appointed by a court to act for someone who is unable to act alone, on matters of succession and trusts, and for the winding up of a company. However, most cases concern debt, divorce and personal injury.

Juries can be used in certain types of Court of Session cases, such as personal injury claims or defamation.

4.2.2 The Inner House

The Inner House is made up of two Divisions, each with five judges. The Lord President of the Court of Session presides over the First Division and the Lord Justice-Clerk presides over the Second Division. An Extra Division of three judges sits frequently to relieve the pressure of business on the court.

Mostly, each Division acts as an appeal court to review decisions of the Outer House judges and of other inferior courts. In practice, each Division normally sits with three judges. Decisions are by a majority, with each judge having one vote. Sometimes, if a case is particularly important or difficult and the court wishes to review a previous decision to resolve the difficulty, a Division can summon additional judges to make up a larger court of five or more judges.

4.3 The House of Lords

The 'House of Lords' is actually the Appellate Committee of the House of Lords, which is made up of Lords of Appeal chosen from the Lord Chancellor, the Lords of Appeal in Ordinary and other peers who have held high judicial office. Informally, they are referred to as the Law Lords; non-lawyer peers do not take part in judicial proceedings.

The House of Lords hears cases at first instance, that is when they are first raised, only in breach of privilege, disputed claims to a peerage and impeachment. It is effectively the final court of appeal from the civil courts, although subject to decisions of the European Court of Justice on European Union law matters.

Normally, five Lords of Appeal sit to hear an appeal; the quorum is three. Usually at least two are Scottish. However, there is no requirement that a Scottish Law Lord must be present to hear a Scottish appeal and in consequence, non-Scottish judges with little or no knowledge of Scots law can decide Scottish appeals.

4.4 The United Kingdom Supreme Court

In October 2009, the jurisdiction of the Appellate Committee of the House of Lords is due to transfer to a new supreme court. The Supreme Court will:

- hear appeals on arguable points of law of general public importance
- act as the final court of appeal in England, Wales and Northern Ireland
- hear appeals from civil cases in Scotland, England, Wales and Northern Ireland
- hear appeals from criminal cases in England, Wales and Northern Ireland

- assume the devolution jurisdiction of the Judicial Committee of the Privy Council, while the Commonwealth jurisdiction of the Council will remain unchanged.

The current Lords of Appeal in Ordinary (the Law Lords) will be the first justices of the 12-member Supreme Court and will remain members of the House of Lords once the court is created. All new judges appointed to the Supreme Court after its creation will not be members of the House of Lords; they will become Justices of the Supreme Court.

4.5   The European Court of Justice

The European Court of Justice (see 1.6.5) exists to ensure compliance with the law in the application and interpretation of the treaties and is the European Union's supreme court. The judges owe their allegiance to the court and not to their home countries.

The Court of First Instance was created in 1989 to strengthen the judicial safeguards available to individuals by introducing a second tier of judicial authority and enabling the Court of Justice to concentrate on its essential task, the uniform interpretation of Community law.

The Court of Justice has one judge from each member state and two judges from one of the larger states. The court may sit either as a whole or with fewer numbers, depending on the type and importance of the case. The Court of First Instance has one judge from each member state. Each court has advocates–general who present preliminary reasoned judgements to the courts.

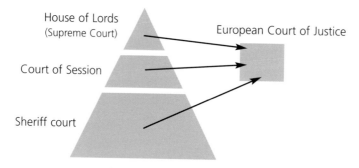

Figure 1. The civil courts (simplified)

Courts of special jurisdiction have jurisdiction in particular kinds of claim only.

The Scottish Land Court deals with agricultural tenancies, crofting tenancies and rent review arbitrations.

The Restrictive Practices Court, which is a United Kingdom court, deals with restrictive and unfair trade practices and claims for the exemption of goods from the rule abolishing resale price maintenance.

The Lands Valuation Appeal Court hears appeals from the decisions of the local Valuation Appeal Committees on the rateable values of commercial property.

The Employment Appeal Tribunal, which by its constituent Act is declared to be a court, has jurisdiction throughout the United Kingdom and hears appeals from employment tribunals.

The Court of Exchequer in Scotland deals with tax disputes.

The Registration of Voters Appeal Court deals with appeals from the sheriff concerning the registration of parliamentary electors.

The Election Petition Court hears petitions to set aside the election of Members of Parliament on the grounds of corruption, illegality and the like.

The Court of the Lord Lyon King of Arms has jurisdiction in disputes over the right to bear coats-of-arms. Prosecutions may be brought to the Lord Lyon Court against the wrongful assumption or use of arms.

The Court of Teinds deals with tithes or tenth parts of harvests once paid by the laity to maintain the church. Teind law is now unimportant and the court's business is almost wholly formal.

4.7   Administrative functions of courts

Both the Court of Session and the sheriff court have certain administrative functions relating to the applications brought before the courts – see 4.1 and 4.21. The sheriff court deals with petitions from creditors for sequestration (the Scottish legal term for personal bankruptcy) and the adoption of children, and deals with applications for the confirmation of executors in respect of the estate of someone who has died.

The Office of the Public Guardian, which is part of the Scottish Court Service, was set up following the passing of the Adults with Incapacity (Scotland) Act 2000. It deals with the appointment of people who take care of the property, financial affairs and personal welfare of adults (in terms of the Act, persons over 16 years old) who are incapable by reason of mental disorder or an inability to communicate. It also administers the Accountant of Court's Office, which supervises judicial factors of the estates of children.

At the time of writing, a wide-ranging review of the provision of civil justice by the courts in Scotland was being carried out. The review will look at the structure, jurisdiction, procedures and working methods of the civil courts and is expected to report by the spring of 2009.

4.8   Further reading

The Scottish Court Service: a comprehensive guide. Available free of charge from the Scottish Court Service, Hayweight House, 23 Lauriston Street, Edinburgh EH3 9DQ, http://www.scotcourts.gov.uk

5

Civil procedure

5.1 Introduction

A civil dispute arises when two or more parties disagree on matters of fact or law or both that affect their legal rights and duties. Most civil disputes are settled by agreement or compromise. When a dispute cannot be settled in this way, it can often only be resolved by taking it before a court or tribunal. However, some disputes may be resolved by more informal methods such as mediation, arbitration or other forms of alternative dispute resolution (see Chapter 6).

Civil procedure (like criminal procedure) is usually adversarial. In other words, it is a legal contest between the two parties, and the judge, or in some cases the jury, decides a case on the basis of the facts alleged and proved by the parties or their lawyers and their legal arguments. The person who starts the case (the pursuer) has to prove it 'on the balance of probabilities' and puts before the court evidence and arguments that support his or her case and entitle him or her to a remedy. The person called to answer the case (the defender) may claim that the pursuer has not proved the case, or submit evidence and arguments to show why the pursuer should not receive what he or she is claiming. The defender also has the option of lodging a counterclaim. If the defender does not appear to defend the case, a 'decree in absence', that is a judicial decision made in someone's absence, may be issued against him or her. The parties can settle a dispute at any stage before a case is decided, either in court or out of court.

In any case that involves the interpretation or validity of European Union law, national courts may, and in some cases they must, suspend the case until the matter has been referred to the European Court of Justice for a ruling. Once the European Court has made a ruling, the case then comes back to the national court, which applies the ruling to the particular facts of the case and decides accordingly. Where the matter comes up in a House of Lords case, which is the ultimate national court of appeal in civil cases, the House of Lords has no option but to refer it to the European Court.

5.2   The Court of Session

The Court of Session has jurisdiction over all civil claims brought in Scotland except in cases where the law places jurisdiction solely with the sheriff court, a court of special jurisdiction (see 4.6) or a statutory tribunal.

Cases brought to the Court of Session are almost always brought as 'actions' or 'petitions'. The object of an action is to enforce a legal right against a defender who resists it or to protect a legal right that the defender is infringing. The object of a petition is generally to obtain from the Court, power to do something or to require something to be done but which the petitioner has no legal right to do, apart from judicial authority.

5.2.1 Actions in the Court of Session

An action in the Court of Session is begun when one party, the pursuer, serves (usually by post) on the other party, the defender, a summons that has been registered and signeted in the offices of the court. The signet is a seal by which certain writs in the name of the Sovereign, including a Court of Session summons, are verified.

The summons or initial writ, that is the legal document that commences the court proceedings against someone, states that the defender should attend court, otherwise a decree in absence may be granted against him or her. Attached to it are: a request to grant the remedy the pursuer wants (for example, payment of a sum of money in reparation for a personal injury caused by the defender); a brief statement of the facts as the pursuer sees them, which, if proved, should be enough to entitle the pursuer to the remedy he or she seeks; and the legal basis for the pursuer's claim.

The defender has a chance to put forward his or her statement of the facts, either accepting or rejecting the pursuer's statement, together with legal arguments in support of his or her own case. Both parties then have an opportunity to adjust their own case in response to the statements, allegations and arguments put forward by the other side. The matter then goes forward for decision by the court.

If the dispute concerns questions of law, there will be a debate in court between lawyers on those legal questions and, if the parties agree about the facts, the court will give its decision granting, or refusing, the remedy sought by the pursuer.

Where there is a dispute about the facts, evidence will be submitted to the judge sitting without a jury or in rare cases, before the judge sitting with a jury.

In civil cases, the jury is twelve. During the selection of the jury, each side in the case has a right to object to a maximum of four potential jurors without giving a reason. The role of the jury is to decide the issue or issues that are put to it, having heard and considered the facts according to the evidence led. At least seven jurors must be satisfied 'on the balance of probabilities' that, for example, the accident to the pursuer was caused by the fault of the defender and, if so, what level of damages should be awarded.

5.2.2 Petitions in the Court of Session

A petition is an application by one side only to the court. Petitions are often used where the petitioner and the respondent to the petition are not in dispute but where the law nevertheless requires the court's approval for some matter. Examples include petitions for the sequestration of an insolvent person, for the liquidation of a company, for an order enabling a person to adopt a child, for the appointment of a judicial factor to administer property, or for the alteration of the purposes of a trust.

Some types of petition, however, can be contentious; for example petitions to vary a trust or petitions for judicial review. A petition is presented to the court, and the court then decides who should receive service or intimation of the petition. Any respondent to the petition may lodge answers in much the same way as any defender to a summons can lodge defences.

The Court of Session also has an inherent equitable power, known the *nobile officium* (its noble office), to provide a remedy where none is available under existing legislation or the rules of common law. Someone wishing to ask the Court of Session to use this power must do so by submitting a petition.

5.3   Sheriff court civil procedure

The procedure followed in the sheriff court depends on the value of the claim. There are three different systems: small claims for claims of £3,000 or less, summary cause for claims over £3,000 and not exceeding £5,000, and ordinary cause for claims over £5,000.

5.3.1 Small claims

The small claims procedure, which deals with claims of £3,000 or less, was introduced in 1988. The rules were revised in 2002 and the current upper limit was introduced for small claims actions raised on or after 14 January 2008.

Although technically part of summary cause procedure, small claims has its own rules and is meant to be faster, simpler, cheaper and more informal. The procedure may be initiated or defended by an ordinary citizen, for example, to recover a consumer debt. However, the majority tend to be raised by large businesses, local authorities, public utilities and mail-order companies.

The procedure is initiated by the pursuer filling in a pre-printed form (the summons) and returning it to court. If the pursuer is an ordinary individual, not a company, the sheriff clerk will send the summons to the person against whom the claim is made.

Although the procedure is intended to be informal, this does not always happen, as complicated questions of law can arise and be dealt with in an adversarial fashion.

5.3.2 Summary cause procedure

Claims valued at between £3,000 and £5,000 are dealt with under summary cause procedure. Certain other types of court action, such as applications for the repossession of property, are also dealt with under the procedure.

Summary cause procedure is generally more complicated than small claims procedure. However, many actions are straightforward and the sheriff has large discretion over procedure. Most claims are for recovery of a debt or repossession of property.

5.3.3 Ordinary cause procedure

Claims valued at over £5,000 are dealt with under ordinary cause procedure.

The procedure in ordinary cause actions is similar to that in actions in the Court of Session (see 5.2.1), but there are time limits which apply in the sheriff court that do not apply in the Court of Session. After a period of adjustment of the written statements, the action then goes to an 'options hearing', where the sheriff decides what the issues in dispute between the parties really are, and what further procedure is needed, bearing in mind the need to progress the case at a reasonable speed.

Most cases relating to family matters, for example, those relating to the end of a marriage or civil partnership, or the residence of children, will need the parties involved in the action to attend the options hearing. This is to see if the parties can agree anything. The sheriff can refer family cases to an appropriate family mediation service (see 6.1). When a case involves children, a child welfare hearing is normally held.

In civil proceedings, jury trial has been abolished in the sheriff court.

5.3.4 Summary and other special applications

The purpose of a summary application, which is regulated by specific rules of court, is to obtain from the sheriff power to do something or require something to be done for which the sheriff's authority is needed. This is usually regulated by statute but in some cases by the common law.

The sheriff court disposes of a wide variety of administrative and miscellaneous matters by this procedure. The procedure in a summary application is at the sheriff's discretion. In other special applications, the procedure is wholly or partly prescribed by statute or act of sederunt (procedural rules made by judges of the Court of Session).

5.3.5 Going to court

An individual who goes to court may always represent him or herself, or be represented by a solicitor, solicitor advocate or an advocate. It is much easier for a person to act on his or her own or with the help of a non-lawyer representative in small claims and summary cause actions than in ordinary cause or Court of Session actions.

In civil proceedings in the sheriff court, a non-lawyer is anyone who is not a solicitor, solicitor advocate, advocate or a person exercising a right to conduct litigation or a right of audience granted by the Lord President of the Court of Session and Scottish Ministers.

The only circumstances in which non-lawyer representation is permitted are:

• Small claims and summary cause actions (first calling only).

• Proceedings under the Debtors (Scotland) Act 1987.

• Proceedings before a sheriff relating to attachment under the Debt Arrangement and Attachment (Scotland) Act 2002.

• In relation to certain aspects of sequestration proceedings under the Bankruptcy (Scotland) Act 1985.

- Proceedings for a time order under the Consumer Credit Act 2006 (from October 2008).

- Where the non-lawyer representative is authorised by a specific piece of legislation to conduct proceedings in the sheriff court in accordance with the terms of that legislation.

5.3.6 Witnesses

In a civil action, the parties to the action are responsible for ensuring that any witnesses they intend to call attend court. They can either be asked to attend on the day of the court hearing or, more formally, be sent a 'citation', that is a summons to attend, and they must attend court at the time and date specified. A citation can only be sent to a prospective witness by a solicitor or sheriff officer. The party calling the witness must instruct the solicitor or sheriff officer to cite the witness and is responsible any fees they may charge and any expenses the witness claims, although these may be recovered by the successful party in an award of expenses.

A party who is not represented by a solicitor will have to assure the court that he or she will be able to pay any witness expenses he or she becomes liable for. That is done by a procedure known as finding caution, and requires a deposit of money to cover the costs. Witnesses must be given at least seven days' notice of the date of the hearing. Special procedures apply where a witness is a child (that is under 16), or a vulnerable witness (that is has a mental disorder, or is experiencing fear or distress in connection with giving evidence in the case). The procedure for the examination of witnesses is described in 9.7.

5.4 Special courts and tribunals

Special courts and tribunals have a wide range of procedures, depending on the purposes for which they were established. Some special courts and tribunals have formal rules of procedure, while many tribunals are informal (see Chapter 7).

5.5 Remedies

The more common civil remedies are:

- Payment – an order to pay a sum of money such as a debt
- Specific implement – an order to do something, for example, to deliver goods or perform a service.
- Interdict – an order prohibiting the commission or continued commission of a legal wrong, for example, against broadcasting an allegedly defamatory statement.
- Declarator – a pronouncement that a particular individual or corporate body has a specific right or duty, for example, that a local authority has a duty to house a homeless person.
- Damages – an order to pay financial compensation for loss or injury caused by fault or neglect, for example, an award of damages for loss caused by breach of contract or personal injuries resulting from fault or neglect.
- Reduction – an order that sets aside as invalid a document that is prejudicial to the pursuer's rights, for example, a will.
- Aliment – an order to provide financial support for a spouse or civil partner, for example, in a divorce or dissolution action.
- Consistorial remedies – judicial separation of two spouses or civil partners, divorce or dissolution.
- Protection – securing the possession of property.

In addition, there are numerous specific remedies provided by statute for specific circumstances. The Court of Session also has the power of judicial review over the decisions of lower courts and tribunals and of government, on the grounds of procedural impropriety, such as the lack of natural justice (for instance, not hearing both sides of a case) or *ultra vires* (acting beyond one's powers) (see Chapter 12), and its *nobile officium* (see 5.2.2).

5.6 Diligence

If a court's order is not obeyed, the pursuer can enforce it through 'diligence'. The essential first step in diligence is a charge – a formal demand for payment – which is served by a messenger-at-arms (for a Court of Session decree) or sheriff officer (for a sheriff court decree) (see 10.5). The common forms of diligence are:

- Arrestment – attaching the funds or property of a debtor that are held by a third party, such as a bank.

- Earnings arrestment – making deductions from a debtor's earnings. There are legal limits to the amount of earnings that can be arrested.

- Attachment – identifying and valuing moveable property owned by and in the possession of a debtor that cannot be disposed of until the debt is paid. If the debt is not paid, attached assets with a value sufficient to cover the debt can be removed and auctioned. It applies only to property kept outwith the debtor's home, and assets required for a profession, trade or business up to a legal limit are exempt. To attach assets in a debtor's home, an exceptional attachment order must be granted.

- Inhibition – preventing the sale of heritable property, that is, land and buildings.

In Scotland, imprisonment for non-payment of debt can only occur for non-payment of aliment.

5.7   Appeals

Most decisions taken by a court or tribunal can be appealed. Appeals may be on a point of fact or law or both. An appeal court can agree with the decision of the lower court, substitute its own judgement, or send the case back to the lower court for further procedure or a final decision, taking the judgement of the appeal court into account.

In civil cases, appeals depend on the court and the procedure used:

- A decision of a judge in the Outer House of the Court of Session can be appealed to the Inner House on a point of law or fact or on the way the judge exercised discretion, and may be further appealed to the House of Lords.

- In small claims, appeal is to the sheriff principal on a point of law only.

- In summary cause actions, appeal is to the sheriff principal on a point of law only, and then to the Inner House of the Court of Session, and finally to the House of Lords.

- In ordinary cause actions, appeal is to the sheriff principal, and then to the Court of Session. On a point of law only, appeal can then be made to the House of Lords.

- Appeals from the decisions of special courts and tribunals depend on the particular court or tribunal involved.

In October 2009, the appeals functions of the House of Lords are due to transfer to the new United Kingdom Supreme Court (see 4.4).

5.8   Fatal accident and sudden death inquiries

Following a fatal accident at work, death in legal custody (for example, in prison or a police station), and other cases of sudden, suspicious or unexplained death, the procurator fiscal may arrange a public inquiry. There are no coroners in Scotland.

Information is collected by the procurator fiscal and presented to a sheriff or sheriff principal. Interested parties may appear personally and take part in the inquiry or may be represented by a solicitor or advocate. Interested parties could include relatives of the person who has died, employers, fellow employees, trade union representatives, and inspectors of factories and mines.

The inquiry is held in public and conducted on the lines of a civil trial. At the end, the sheriff makes a decision in which he or she sets out the circumstances affecting the death, including any precautions that may have avoided it and any defects that may have contributed to it. Decisions do not usually include findings of fault against anyone and may include recommendations for safer practices.

The decision cannot be used in any subsequent civil or criminal proceedings arising from the accident and witnesses are not required to answer any question that may incriminate them.

At the time of writing, fatal accident and sudden death inquiries in Scotland were under review.

5.9 Further reading

Ervine, W Cowan H, *Small Claims Handbook*, 2nd edition. W Green, Edinburgh, 2003. £52.

Small Claims and Summary Cause guidance: http://www.scotcourts.gov.uk

6

Alternative Dispute Resolution

6.1 Introduction

Alternative dispute resolution (ADR) provides alternative ways of resolving disputes, usually outwith the courts. ADR may be used in family, commercial, consumer and community disputes. The most common forms of ADR are mediation and arbitration.

6.2 Mediation

Mediation is a process of structured negotiations where the disputing parties are assisted by a neutral third party to reach their own resolution to their conflict. Mediation is most often used in family, neighbourhood and commercial disputes, and can be used in court actions, in schools, including peer mediation, in disputes in the work place and employment, in environment and planning disputes, and in disputes over additional educational support needs.

Examples of when meditation may be used include:

• The Children (Scotland) Act 1995 allows a court to refer a couple to mediation at any time during a family action where there are children.

• In civil disputes, the in-court mediation service in Edinburgh sheriff court can help people to resolve problems without going to a full hearing before a sheriff or judge. Following an evaluation of pilot in-court mediation services in Glasgow and Aberdeen sheriff courts, further services may be developed.

• The Education (Additional Support for Learning) (Scotland) Act 2004 includes a requirement for education authorities to have in place arrangements for independent mediation to resolve disputes between parents and the authority or school or both about a child who has additional support needs.

Mediation activities may be funded in a number of ways. For example, within the commercial sphere, it is normal practice for the disputing parties to share equally the costs of mediation. Legal aid is available for eligible partners who wish to use mediation to resolve issues arising from divorce, dissolution or separation (see 13.3). Legal aid is also available for mediation in non-family civil disputes.

6.3   Arbitration

The parties to arbitration agree the procedure, with the degree of formality influenced by the balance of fact or law involved. Lawyers may be involved, there may be legal arguments, inspections may be made of the subject matter or premises in dispute, or experts may be consulted, depending on the particular arbitration.

Consumers or small businesses (that is with ten or fewer employees) can use the Independent Consumer Arbitration Service in disputes with companies registered with the service.

In going to arbitration, the parties agree to exclude the jurisdiction of the courts. While a court may state an opinion on a point of law referred to it during arbitration, there is no appeal from the arbiter's decision. However, a court may reduce an award where, for example, it decides there has been a conflict of interest, or the arbiter has dealt with a point outwith the terms of reference, or there has been a denial of natural justice.

The existing law on arbitration in Scotland is nearly all uncodified common law, and the powers and duties of an arbitrator in any particular case may not be clear, unless they have previously been set out in an arbitration agreement. At the time of writing, the Scottish Government was consulting on a proposed Arbitration (Scotland) Bill, which aims to put the majority of the general Scots law of arbitration into a single statute.

6.4   Additional reading

Resolving Disputes without Going to Court. Scottish Executive, 2006. Available free at:
http://www.scotland.gov.uk/Resource/Doc/47060/0025017.pdf

Tribunals

7.1 Introduction

Tribunals exercise judicial or quasi-judicial functions in that they exist to resolve disputes about the law or the technical application of the law, but they are not technically courts of law. The number of tribunals has grown considerably in recent years. They are perceived as having advantages over courts in being able to deal with cases more informally, more cheaply, more quickly, and with specific expertise.

There is a wide range of different kinds of tribunals, varying in the kind of dispute that they deal with, how they are administered, their membership and the formality of their procedures.

Tribunals deal with disputes between individuals and public authorities. For example, the Social Security and Child Support Appeals Tribunal hears appeals against Department of Work and Pensions decisions on eligibility for certain social security benefits, HM Revenue and Customs decisions on tax credits and local authority decisions on housing benefit and council tax benefit. But some tribunals deal with disputes between private individuals or organisations, for example, employment tribunals and the Lands Tribunal for Scotland.

Some tribunals are organised on a United Kingdom basis. For example, the Social Security and Child Support Commissioners deal with applications for leave to appeal and appeals from social security, medical, disability and child support appeal tribunals throughout the United Kingdom. Others, such as children's hearings and the Mental Health Tribunal for Scotland, operate only in Scotland. Some are administered by local authorities, for example, education appeal committees, and valuation appeal committees, which hear council tax appeals.

The composition of tribunals varies. Often there is a legally-qualified chairman or tribunal judge with two other members who have specific expertise, although some social security tribunals operate with a legally-qualified chairman alone. Some tribunals are composed entirely of non-lawyers; for example, children's hearings.

Sometimes a dispute may be appealed through a hierarchy of tribunals. For example, certain questions of income tax from the Inspector of Taxes to the Special or General Commissioners of Income Tax, or a decision of an immigration officer to an adjudicator to the Asylum and Immigration Tribunal. Appeals on a point of law may be taken to the Court of Session from most tribunals. Where there is no specific right of appeal, a decision of a tribunal may be brought before the Court of Session by the procedure of judicial review (see Chapter 12), but only on the grounds of refusal to exercise jurisdiction, acting in excess of jurisdiction, procedural irregularity or breach of natural justice.

The Administrative Justice and Tribunals Council, which has a Scottish Committee based in Edinburgh, supervises most tribunals and keeps under review the administrative justice system as a whole. Certain tribunals that deal with disciplinary matters in particular professions (such as the Scottish Solicitors Discipline Tribunal (see 15.2.4) and the General Medical Council) are not subject to supervision by the Administrative Justice and Tribunals Council.

The Scottish Committee has a particular remit in relation to administrative justice and tribunals in Scotland, including those United Kingdom-wide tribunals that sit in Scotland, and some twenty tribunals that are constituted under separate Scottish legislation. These cover a wide range of subjects including education appeal committees, mental health tribunals for Scotland, additional support needs tribunals for Scotland and National Health Service discipline committees in Scotland.

Two examples of particular tribunals operating in Scotland are given below.

In Scotland, children under the age of 16 who may need care and protection or who have committed an offence can be brought to a children's hearing, which is a statutory non-lawyer tribunal composed of three members of the children's panel for the local authority area. Children under 16 are only considered for prosecution in the courts where serious offences, such as murder, rape or assault to the danger of life are involved.

A child who may be in need of compulsory measures of care must be referred to the reporter to the children's panel, who is an independent official. If the reporter decides to refer a child to a hearing, the child may be brought before a hearing on a number of grounds. These include being beyond the control of any relevant person; falling into bad associations or being exposed to moral danger; suffering through lack of parental care; being a victim of physical injury or sexual abuse; failing to attend school; having committed an offence.

The children's hearing is informal and in private. Its purpose is to decide whether the child is in need of compulsory measures of care. If it decides such measures are appropriate, it will impose a supervision requirement that can be renewed until the child is 18. The requirement may be that the child lives at home under the supervision of the social work department, or that the child should live away from home with relatives, foster carers or in a residential home. A hearing cannot fine the child or the parents.

There is a right of appeal on a point of law only to a sheriff and from there to the Court of Session. It is also possible to appeal to the Court of Session if the proper procedures have not been followed.

Employment tribunals have jurisdiction over a wide range of issues connected with employment including, for example, claims for equal pay, complaints about sex, racial or disability discrimination, failure to pay maternity pay, failure to provide full pay, unfair dismissal, unreasonable exclusion from a trade union. An employment tribunal has three members – a legally-qualified tribunal judge and two non-lawyer members, one with an employer's background and the other an employee's background (although in some circumstances the tribunal judge may sit and hear cases on his or her own).

Appeal on a question of law may be made to the Employment Appeal Tribunal. The tribunal (see 4.6) is made up of judges of the English High Court, one or more judges of the Court of Session, and non-lawyer members with specialist knowledge of employment relations.

7.4 Further reading

Children's Hearing System: http://www.childrens-hearings.co.uk

Making a claim to an employment tribunal. Employment Tribunals, 2006. Available at: http://www.employmenttribunals.gov.uk/about_us/document/Making_a_claim.pdf

Norrie, Kenneth, *Children's Hearings in Scotland*. W Green, Edinburgh, 2005. £56.

The criminal courts

8.1 Introduction

In Scotland, crimes are prosecuted in the district or justice of the peace court, the sheriff court and the High Court of Justiciary. The Crown Office and Procurator Fiscal Service is the sole public prosecution service in Scotland – private prosecutions are extremely rare (see 9.3). Generally, the district or justice of the peace court deals with minor offences, and the sheriff court deals with more serious offences. The most serious offences, such as rape and murder, are dealt with in the High Court.

The more serious crimes are tried under solemn procedure, where a judge sits with a jury, which can be in the sheriff court or the High Court. Less serious offences are tried under summary procedure, before a sheriff sitting alone, or before either one or three justices of the peace (in a district or justice of the peace court). Most criminal prosecutions in Scotland are summary cases.

8.2 The district court

District courts handle prosecutions of certain minor offences committed within the district. The courts are presided over by non-lawyer justices of the peace. In Glasgow, there are also legally-qualified stipendiary (that is, salaried) magistrates who sit in the district court.

The jurisdiction of the court includes all statutory offences that are capable of being tried summarily. The court has no jurisdiction over children under 16 years of age.

The powers of punishment of a district court are limited to up to 60 days' imprisonment or a fine of £2,500 or both, although a stipendiary magistrate has the same sentencing power as a sheriff has under summary procedure.

8.3   The justice of the peace court

Until March 2008, local authorities administered district courts, except those in Orkney and Shetland, while the Scottish Court Service administered the Court of Session, the High Court and the sheriff courts. Under the Criminal Proceedings etc (Reform) (Scotland) Act 2007, district courts are being replaced by justice of the peace courts administered by the Scottish Court Service (see 11.2). Sheriffdoms will undergo unification for these purposes and as each one does so, district courts will be disestablished and justice of the peace courts will be established in their place. In most cases the location of the court will remain unchanged.

The provision of stipendiary magistrates in Glasgow and the courts' jurisdiction and sentencing powers remain unchanged.

High Court and Court of Criminal Appeal

European Court of Justice

Sheriff court

District court / justice of the peace court

Figure 2. The criminal courts (simplified)

8.4   The sheriff court

The sheriff court deals with more serious cases than the district or justice of the peace court. It can deal with any offences committed within the sheriffdom that are not reserved for the

High Court (rape, murder, attempted murder, etc.), including those that may be dealt with by the district or justice of the peace court.

In cases tried under summary procedure, a sheriff's powers of punishment are limited to 12 months' imprisonment or a fine of up to £10,000, although these powers may be limited or widened for offences by statute.

Solemn procedure is used in more serious cases. Where solemn cases are tried in the sheriff court, the sheriff can impose a maximum sentence of five years' imprisonment or an unlimited fine. If a sheriff feels that in any particular case his or her powers are too limited, the convicted person can be sent to the High Court for sentence.

A number of specialist criminal courts have been established in recent years. Pilot drug courts, which are due to run until 2009, operate in Glasgow and Fife sheriff courts. These courts have powers to make probation orders or drug treatment and testing orders, where offenders are subject to drug testing and the orders to regular review, as alternatives to custody. Drug treatment and testing orders are also available in other sheriff courts. Glasgow sheriff court also has a pilot domestic violence court, where a dedicated sheriff deals with domestic violence cases, and alleged violent partners are 'fast-tracked' through the system by procurators fiscal.

8.5   The High Court of Justiciary

The High Court of Justiciary is Scotland's supreme criminal court. There is no appeal from it to the House of Lords. It was established in 1672, replacing the Court of the Justiciar. The judges are the same as those in the Court of Session but wear different robes.

The person appointed as Lord President of the Court of Session is also head of the High Court, but there he or she is known as the Lord Justice-General. The second most senior judge is known as the Lord Justice-Clerk. The High Court is both a trial court and a court of appeal.

As a trial court, the High Court sits in cities and larger towns throughout Scotland. Edinburgh and Glasgow both have permanent High Court buildings. Throughout the rest of the country, the High Court sits in local sheriff court buildings where they are large enough to accommodate it, including Stirling, Oban, Inverness, Aberdeen, Dundee, Perth, Dumfries, Jedburgh and Ayr, or at any convenient town near where the crime being tried was carried out.

The High Court has jurisdiction over all of Scotland, and covers all types of crime not specifically reserved to another court. Only the High Court can deal with allegations of treason, murder, rape, incest, certain offences under the Official Secrets Act, obstruction of officers of the court (called 'deforcement of messengers'), and breach of duty by magistrates.

Normally, only one judge sits at a trial but exceptionally, in cases of importance or difficulty, two or more, usually three, may sit. There is always a jury. The prosecution is conducted by a law officer or advocate depute (see 9.3) and the accused person is defended by an advocate or a solicitor advocate.

As an appeal court, the High Court sits only in Edinburgh. All appeals from the district court, the justice of the peace court (see 8.3), the sheriff court and the High Court come before this court, and it hears appeals in cases referred to it by the Scottish Criminal Cases Review Commission (see 9.10). In general, appeals against conviction or against conviction and sentence are heard by three judges and appeals against sentence are considered by two judges. The High Court also has power to deal with unusual or unforeseen circumstances in the exercise of its equitable power, known as the *nobile officium* (see 9.9).

8.6   Further reading

The Scottish Court Service: a comprehensive guide. Available free from Scottish Court Service, Hayweight House, 23 Lauriston Street, Edinburgh EH3 9DQ, http://www.scotcourts.gov.uk

Criminal procedure

9.1   Introduction

Following the Union of 1707, Scottish criminal justice continued to be very different from that in England and Wales. The Scotland Act 1998 provided protection for the system following devolution in 1999 by entrenching the Lord Advocate as head of the systems of criminal prosecutions and investigation of deaths.

9.2   Criminal investigation

The procurator fiscal has responsibility at local level for the investigation and prosecution of crime. In practice, the police or a statutory reporting agency, such as HM Revenue and Customs, carry out the initial investigation.

If a person is arrested, he or she must be charged with a crime and cautioned that he or she need say nothing but that anything he or she does say may be noted and used in evidence. Failure to caution a suspect or unreasonable harshness in questioning by the police may result in any alleged confession being held to be inadmissible at a subsequent trial.

The police must take all precautions against the unreasonable and unnecessary detention of a suspected person. In most cases, someone who has been charged is then released, except where the police take the view that the accused should remain in custody until the next court day.

The police can then use direct measures, such as warnings or fixed penalties, although in most cases a report that the accused has been charged with a particular offence and a summary of the evidence is then sent to the procurator fiscal. In due course, if the procurator fiscal decides to go ahead with a prosecution, the accused person has to appear in court to answer the charges.

If the procurator fiscal is satisfied that a crime has been committed and that there is sufficient evidence of that crime, he or she will consider what action is required in the public interest. This will include taking no action, the use of an alternative to prosecution or prosecution. He or she has a statutory duty, in terms of the Scotland Act 1998, to act in a way that is compatible with the convention rights as defined in the Human Rights Act 1998. The procurator fiscal's discretion to prosecute or not is a principal feature of the system. There is no rule of law in Scotland that a criminal offence must be prosecuted. However, once a complaint has been made, it is entirely at the procurator fiscal's discretion whether a case is continued or discontinued.

9.2.1 Alternatives to prosecution

There are a number of alternatives to prosecution, also known as 'direct measures':

- The procurator fiscal may warn someone who has been reported by the police that his or her behaviour is unacceptable and that any repetition will result in prosecution.

- In certain minor cases, where there is an identifiable victim, a background of conflict between the two parties, or an indication that the accused is in a position to make amends, the procurator fiscal may arrange supervised reparation or mediation between the alleged offender and victim.

- For an offence triable by a district or justice of the peace court, the procurator fiscal may offer the offender the option of paying a fine (a fiscal fine) or paying compensation to the victim of the alleged crime. Refusal of an offer will result in prosecution.

- Since June 2008, an offer of a fiscal work order – a short period of unpaid work of up to 50 hours – is being piloted in some areas for two years. Refusal of the offer will result in prosecution.

- A police officer may offer an 'on the spot' fixed penalty for low-level antisocial behaviour.

- For certain minor road-traffic offences, a police officer or traffic warden may issue a fixed-penalty notice. Failure to pay will result in the penalty being recovered as a fine.

- In the case of other minor road-traffic offences, the procurator fiscal may offer the alternative of paying a fixed penalty. If such an offer is accepted, and payment made, no prosecution is brought. In the case of an endorsable offence, the relevant penalty points are also added to the offender's driving licence.

Acceptance of a direct measure is not a conviction. However, an accepted direct measure can be disclosed to the court as if it was a previous conviction, if the alleged offender is convicted of another offence within two years.

Even where there appears to be sufficient evidence to prosecute, the procurator fiscal is entitled to decide not to prosecute if the offence is trivial or it is otherwise not in the public interest.

9.3 The system of public prosecution: the Crown Office and procurators fiscal

The Lord Advocate is the ministerial head of the Crown Office and Procurator Fiscal Service, and head of the systems of criminal prosecution and the investigation of deaths. His or her appointment is political and may change with a change of the Scottish Government. While the Lord Advocate is accountable to the Scottish Parliament for the operation of the department in his or her charge, he or she is not required to justify any particular exercise of his or her discretion as prosecutor to anyone, including the courts and the Scottish Parliament. The independence of the Lord Advocate in his or her capacity as the head of the systems of criminal prosecution and the investigation of deaths in Scotland is preserved by the Scotland Act 1998.

The Crown Office and Procurator Fiscal Service is responsible for the preparation of prosecutions in the High Court, the sheriff court, the district court and the justice of the peace court (see 8.3) in Scotland. The Crown Office is responsible for the legal and administrative direction of the procurator fiscal service. Ultimate responsibility for criminal prosecution and the investigation of deaths rests with the Lord Advocate.

The system in Scotland is one of public prosecution. Private prosecution, where the victim undertakes a prosecution rather than the Crown, although rare is possible but requires the agreement of the Lord Advocate.

9.4   Summary and solemn procedure

In criminal court cases, more serious cases are prosecuted under solemn procedure, on 'indictment', either before a sheriff and jury or a High Court judge and jury. Some very serious crimes, such as murder, attempted murder, rape and attempted rape, must be prosecuted under solemn procedure and may only be prosecuted in the High Court.

Summary cases are tried before a sheriff without a jury in the sheriff court, or before a magistrate or justices of the peace in the district court or justice of the peace court (see 8.3). As with civil cases, criminal cases involve each side presenting its evidence to a judge, and a jury if there is one. A fundamental principle of criminal law is that the accused person is presumed innocent and the onus of proof is with the prosecution. The standard of proof is 'proof beyond reasonable doubt', which is a higher test than the 'balance of probabilities' test required in civil cases.

9.4.1 Bail

Under summary and solemn procedure an accused person is entitled to be released on bail. It is at the discretion of the courts to grant bail. In determining whether it is appropriate for bail to be granted, the courts will take account of a number of factors including the administration of justice and protecting the public from the accused being at large. An accused person and the prosecutor have a right of appeal to the High Court against a decision of a sheriff in relation to bail at various stages in the proceedings.

If someone is released on bail this is subject to a set of conditions designed to ensure that the accused will be available for enquiry, will appear in court when required, will not commit an offence while on bail and will not interfere with witnesses or obstruct justice. A deposit of money is not usually required, but is possible in special circumstances.

9.5   Summary procedure

In most summary cases, the police will not arrest the person charged with the crime. The accused person will be cited, that is summoned, and sent a 'complaint', setting out where and when he or she must attend court, the accused person's name and address and a description of the alleged offence or offences he or she is accused of.

9.5.1 Pleading diet

Usually someone accused of a crime must appear personally to plead guilty or not guilty. Someone pleading guilty may be sentenced there and then, and if the judge is considering a prison sentence the accused person **must** be present. If an accused person pleads not guilty a trial date will be fixed, when the prosecution will have to prove their case.

It may be possible for an accused person to tender a plea of guilty or not guilty by letter or through a solicitor, although in the event of a plea of guilty the court may defer sentence for the accused to appear personally. Where a plea of guilty is tendered, the court will have regard to the stage at which it is tendered in deciding on any discount to the sentence in return for an early plea.

9.5.2 Intermediate diet

Between the pleading hearing and the trial, an additional hearing, the 'intermediate diet', is held. The accused person must attend, and is asked whether he or she still continues to plead not guilty.

If, at the intermediate diet, the accused person changes his or her plea to guilty, the judge may sentence him or her there and then but can also defer sentence to a later diet after consideration of a social enquiry report about the accused person.

9.5.3 Trial

At the trial, the accused person may be represented by a solicitor, an advocate or a solicitor-advocate, or may represent himself or herself. The accused person will be asked again whether he or she is pleading not guilty, or may plead guilty to a modified charge. If pleading guilty, sentence will be passed once the judge hears any 'pleas in mitigation' and considers the accused person's previous convictions, if any. If the accused person continues to plead not guilty, evidence is led, first by the procurator fiscal, for the prosecution, then by the defence.

The judge has to decide whether he or she considers that the prosecution has proved the case beyond all reasonable doubt. Normally the decision is pronounced at once. If it is 'not guilty' or 'not proven' the accused person is discharged. The effect in both cases is the same – the accused person is immune from further prosecution in relation to the offence. If the accused person is found guilty, then any previous convictions and pleas in mitigation are considered before sentence is passed.

Where the accused person is in custody, a trial must begin within 40 days of the commencement of the complaint being brought to court. If this does not happen, the accused person is freed and is immune from further prosecution for the offence.

9.6 Solemn procedure

In more serious cases, the procurator fiscal may decide that the offence should be prosecuted 'on indictment', that is, under solemn procedure. In these cases, he or she presents a 'petition' to a sheriff which names the accused person, states the charge and seeks warrant to arrest the accused if the accused has not already been arrested. This petition is also a warrant to allow the police to search premises occupied by the accused, cite witnesses for precognition (a statement or record of evidence they may be expected to give) with the procurator fiscal and examine the accused.

9.6.1 Pre-trial procedure

Once the accused person has had an opportunity of consulting a solicitor, he or she may go before a sheriff for judicial examination, where the procurator fiscal can ask questions about his or her response to the charge, any confession alleged to have been made and questions that might obtain admissions about the offence from the accused or obtain information about his or her intended defence. A record of the examination may be used in evidence at a subsequent trial.

If the case is to proceed, the accused is served with an indictment, setting out the offences charged and a list of the evidence to be led at the trial, such as medical reports, and the names of Crown witnesses. The accused person is cited in the indictment to appear on a particular date at the court for a preliminary hearing (known as the 'first diet' in cases before a sheriff and jury) before his or her trial. This is to ensure that the parties are ready for trial on the appointed date. At this hearing, the court can also deal with any objections raised by the accused, or consider any special defence. Objections that can be raised at this stage include, for example, that the crime in the indictment does not amount to a crime in terms of the law of Scotland, and special defences include alibi, self-defence, incrimination (that is, someone else committed the crime), and insanity.

There are strict rules in Scots law that prevent an accused person spending an unduly long period in custody before trial. Where an accused person is in custody and proceedings are being taken in the High Court, the preliminary hearing must take place before the 110th day in custody. At the preliminary hearing, the judge will fix a trial date within a window of 30 days so that the trial must take place within 140 days. If these time limits are not met, the accused will have the right to apply to the court for bail. If bail is granted, a prosecution must take place within 12 months. Where an accused is on bail and he or she is to be tried in the High Court, there must be a preliminary hearing by the 11th month and the trial within 12 months. If the 12-month time limit is not met, the accused will be forever free from prosecution of the crime charged. The prosecutor can apply to the court to have these time limits extended.

9.6.2 Trial

Juries are involved in all criminal trials under solemn procedure, where the jury is made up of 15 members of the public. Each side is allowed to object to individual jurors if they have a good reason, for instance, that they know the accused. The trial then proceeds in a similar way to a summary case, the main difference being that the prosecution has to convince the jury, not the judge, of the guilt of the accused person beyond reasonable doubt.

The jury considers the evidence in the case and its verdict on the guilt or innocence of the accused. The jury can decide a verdict by a majority, and the verdict can be guilty, not proven or not guilty. To reach a verdict of guilty, at least eight jurors have to vote for this. Where the verdict is guilty, the Crown will normally ask the judge to pass sentence. At that stage the Crown advises the judge of any previous convictions that it wishes the judge to take into account in deciding the sentence.

The defence can make a plea in mitigation on behalf of the accused person. The judge then passes sentence, either immediately or after consideration of social enquiry reports about the accused person. A sheriff can refer the case to the High Court for sentence if it is felt that any sentence he or she can pass is inadequate.

9.6.3 Jurors

Potential jurors are selected at random from the electoral register. They must be between the ages of 18 and 65, ordinarily resident in the United Kingdom for at least five years, and registered as an elector. Certain individuals are ineligible or disqualified, and others may be excused jury duty.

Jurors must consider the evidence presented by each side and, subject to directions in matters of law by the presiding judge or sheriff, reach a verdict on one or more matters of fact or of mixed fact and law. In a criminal case, at least eight jurors must be satisfied 'beyond reasonable doubt' that the accused committed the crime charged.

9.7 Witnesses

A person who is cited as a witness in a criminal trial must attend court at the time and date specified. He or she has a duty to cooperate with 'both sides', that is, to give a statement to the procurator fiscal and the defence.

Every sheriff court and High Court has a witness service to provide support and advice to witnesses and their families in criminal cases.

Special procedures apply where a witness is a child (under 16), or a vulnerable witness (that is, has a mental disorder, or is experiencing fear or distress in connection with giving evidence in the case). These may include: a screen in the courtroom; a television link outwith the courtroom; a supporter; a prior statement previously given by the witness; or evidence taken by a commissioner.

9.8 Sentences

Any person convicted of a criminal offence may receive the following sentences:

• a deferred sentence for a period of time, normally on condition that the offender is of good behaviour and sometimes with other conditions, such as attending counselling or repaying money. Under a pilot programme, a structured deferred sentence may be given to certain offenders. Their involvement in the programme is taken into account and those who participate are less likely to be given a custodial sentence;

• a fine;

• an admonition (a warning);

• a period of imprisonment or detention in a young offenders' institution or, if a child, detention in a place and under such conditions as the Scottish Ministers may direct;

- a community-service order;

- probation;

- a drug treatment and testing order, which involves mandatory regular testing and treatment for offenders whose drug misuse is the cause of their offending (Note: this order is also available as an alternative to prosecution – see 8.4);

- a restriction of liberty order, which requires, by means of electronic monitoring, an offender to remain in a specified place (or alternatively to stay away from a specified location);

- a compensation order, which requires the convicted person to pay compensation to the victim, and can be combined with another penalty.

Failure to pay a fine can result in a range of enforcement actions being taken by fines enforcement officers (see 10.6), or imprisonment or a 'supervised attendance order' being imposed. The court can also make an absolute discharge, although this is recorded and may be treated as a previous conviction if the offender re-offends.

The maximum amount of a fine or period of imprisonment is limited in summary procedure. In solemn procedure, the only limits for fines are those that are defined in statute for crimes created by statute.

9.9   Appeals

Anyone convicted of a criminal offence in a summary case can appeal against conviction or sentence or both. Someone who has pled guilty can still appeal against the sentence imposed. The Crown can also appeal in summary proceedings but only on a point of law against an acquittal or a sentence passed. The right of appeal is subject to the granting of leave to appeal by the High Court.

The High Court can send the case back to the original court with directions, agree with the original verdict or set aside the verdict. If it sets aside the verdict, it can quash the conviction, substitute an amended verdict of guilty, or grant authority for a new prosecution.

In solemn procedure, there are broadly similar rules for appeals. However, the Lord Advocate has the right to refer a case resulting in an acquittal to the High Court for a decision on a point of law (although that does not affect the acquittal), and the Crown has a right of appeal against sentence on the grounds of undue leniency. If the appeal court agrees, the sentence can be increased.

Like the Court of Session, the High Court has an equitable power, its *nobile officium*, which it may use to deal with unusual or unforeseen circumstances, or where there is no common law or statutory remedy and no other form of review appears possible or appropriate, or to avoid deadlock, injustice or oppression. It is not an alternative to other forms of appeal.

9.10   The Scottish Criminal Cases Review Commission

The Scottish Criminal Cases Review Commission is a statutory body set up under the Criminal Procedure (Scotland) Act 1995 to review alleged miscarriages of justice in Scotland. If the commission believes that a miscarriage of justice may have occurred in a criminal conviction or sentence in a Scottish court – and it is the interests of justice that a reference should be made – it can refer the case to the Court of Criminal Appeal for review. It will then be heard in the same way as any other appeal.

9.11   The Criminal Injuries Compensation Authority

The Criminal Injuries Compensation Authority was set up under the Criminal Injuries Compensation Act 1995 to administer the tariff-based Criminal Injuries Compensation Scheme that came into effect for all applications from 1 April 1996.

The scheme deals with claims for compensation, in certain circumstances, from victims of crimes of violence and from people hurt as a result of attempts to arrest offenders or prevent offences. A victim includes a dependant of someone who dies as a result of a criminal injury.

Decisions taken by the authority may be appealed to the Criminal Injuries Compensation Appeals Panel, whose members are legally qualified and are appointed by the Lord Chancellor.

9.12   Further reading

Compensation for victims of violent crime: a short guide to the Criminal Injuries Compensation Scheme. Criminal Injuries Compensation Authority, 2007. Available at: http://www.cica.gov.uk

Gane, C H W & Stoddart, C N, *Casebook on Scottish Criminal Law*, 3rd edition. W Green, Edinburgh, 2001. £46.50.

Jones, T H & Christie G A, *Criminal Law*, 4th edition. W Green, Edinburgh, 2008. £36.

Crown Office and Procurator Fiscal Service:
http://www.crownoffice.gov.uk

The personnel of the law

10.1 Judges

The judiciary in Scotland has two distinctive characteristics. First, in civil and criminal litigation, far greater use is made of full-time legally qualified judges than elsewhere in the United Kingdom, where non-lawyer magistrates play a greater role in family law and summary criminal cases. Nevertheless, many prosecutions in Scotland for minor offences are dealt with in district courts and justice of the peace courts. Second, in contrast to the general practice elsewhere in Europe, professional judges are drawn from legal practitioners, rather than persons specially trained to be judges throughout their careers.

10.1.1 Judges in the superior courts

The judges of the Court of Session are the senior permanent judges and technically they are Senators of the College of Justice. The Sovereign makes appointments to the Court of Session, although in practice the Lord President of the Court of Session and the Lord Justice-Clerk are nominated by the Prime Minister on the recommendation of the First Minister. The Prime Minister can only put forward candidates nominated by the First Minister. The Prime Minister also makes recommendations for the appointment of the two Scottish judges in the House of Lords. When the United Kingdom Supreme Court begins work (see 4.4), new justices will be appointed by a selection committee comprising the President and Deputy President of the Supreme Court and members of the appointment bodies for England, Wales, Scotland and Northern Ireland.

Those eligible to be appointed as Senators are sheriffs, sheriffs principal and advocates of five years' standing, writers to the Signet of ten years' standing who have passed the examination in civil law two years before taking up their seat on the bench and solicitor advocates with five years' right of audience in the Court of Session and the High Court of Justiciary. At the time of writing there were proposals to extend eligibility for appointment to those who have practiced as solicitor advocates in either the Court of Session or the High Court of Justiciary (removing the need to have held rights of audience in both the civil and criminal Supreme courts). They are appointed by the Sovereign on the recommendation of the First Minister, following consultation with the Lord President. An independent Judicial Appointments Board for Scotland considers applications from individuals seeking appointment to this judicial office and makes recommendations to the First Minister. On appointment, they take the courtesy title of 'Lord' or 'Lady' followed by their surname or a territorial title (Lord Rodger, Lady Smith, Lord Sutherland). They are not members of the House of Lords, although some have been made life peers.

Senators appointed prior to 31 March 1995 must retire at the age of 75. Those appointed after that date must retire at the age of 70, but they are eligible to continue to sit as retired judges until they are 75. They can be removed from office (see 15.4.2).

Temporary judges may be appointed by the First Minister, following consultation with the Lord President, from among those eligible to be appointed as Senators. The Lord President may also, with the agreement of the First Minister, appoint retired judges to sit but such appointments must come to an end when the individual reaches the age of 75.

The Lord President of the Court of Session, Scotland's most senior judge, is also the Lord Justice-General of the High Court of Justiciary, and all Court of Session judges are also High Court judges. Temporary judges of the Court of Session are also temporary judges of the High Court.

10.1.2 Sheriffs

Sheriffs, including sheriffs principal, are appointed by the Sovereign on the recommendation of the First Minster, who must first consult the Lord President of the Court of Session. Those eligible for appointment as sheriffs are advocates and solicitors of at least ten years' standing. Sheriffs appointed prior to 31 March 1995 must retire at the age of 72. Those appointed after that date must retire at the age of 70. They can be removed from office (see 15.4.3).

Floating sheriffs are permanent full-time sheriffs appointed to sit wherever required throughout Scotland's 49 sheriff courts. They can be removed from office (see 15.4.3).

Part-time sheriffs are appointed by Scottish Ministers to sit as and where necessary to assist with the pressure of business and provide cover for part-time sheriffs who may be away on official business or annual or sick leave. There is provision for up to 80 part-time sheriffs at any one time. They are usually practising solicitors or advocates and may be appointed for up to five years. They do not sit in a court where they would normally appear as a practitioner. They can be removed from office (see 15.4.3).

The Judicial Appointments Board for Scotland considers applications from those seeking appointment to these offices and makes recommendations to the First Minister.

10.1.3 Justices of the peace in the district courts

District courts are presided over by non-lawyer justices of the peace, except in Glasgow where there are also salaried stipendiary magistrates. Stipendiary magistrates are appointed by the local authority from solicitors or advocates of at least five years' standing. 'Full justices' are appointed by the First Minister in the name of the Sovereign and on the recommendation of local justices of the peace advisory committees. They can be removed from office (see 15.4.4). District courts are being replaced by justice of the peace courts (see 8.3).

Local authorities may also nominate their members to serve as 'signing justices'. They do not sit in court but are available for signing warrants, etc.

At the age of 70, all justices are put on the 'supplemental list' and are available only for signing duties.

10.1.4 Justices of the peace in justice of the peace courts

In March 2008, a programme of court unification began by replacing district courts with justice of the peace courts under the administration of the Scottish Court Service. The programme is due for completion by October 2009. Scottish Ministers will appoint justices of the peace for five years on the recommendation of the justice of the peace advisory committee for the local sheriffdom. Appointments can be renewed until they each the age of 70. Signing justices will be retained. All new justices of the peace must undergo a course of training approved by the Lord President before they are appointed, and all current justices must attend a training course approved by the Lord President within two years of taking up appointment. They can be removed from office (see 15.4.4).

10.2 The public prosecutors

The Lord Advocate is the principal law officer of the Crown in Scotland. He or she is assisted by the Solicitor General for Scotland and a number of advocates depute who are the public prosecutors in the High Court. Advocates depute are appointed by the Lord Advocate from practising advocates and are known collectively as 'Crown Counsel'. They devote almost all their practice to Crown work and during the period of their appointment do not engage in any criminal defence work. Crown Counsel work along with a small permanent staff of civil servants, headed by the Crown Agent, in the Crown Office in Edinburgh.

The procurators fiscal are the public prosecutors in the sheriff, district and justice of the peace courts. They are full-time civil servants, independent of the judiciary. They must be advocates or solicitors, and are usually solicitors. The police report details of a crime to the procurator fiscal, who has absolute discretion whether to prosecute, subject to the general direction and control of the Crown Office.

The legal profession in Scotland has two branches: advocates (who correspond to barristers elsewhere in the United Kingdom) and solicitors. A person can move from one branch to another but cannot simultaneously be a member of both. There are about 680 advocates and 10,150 solicitors in Scotland.

10.3.1 Advocates

Members of the Faculty of Advocates are those who have been admitted to practise before the Court of Session. They can also present cases in the other superior courts in Scotland, the House of Lords, the United Kingdom Supreme Court when it comes into being, the Judicial Committee of the Privy Council, the European Court of Justice, the European Court of Human Rights and a wide range of tribunals, enquiries and other such proceedings. They can also appear before all the lower courts in Scotland. The Dean, who is its elected leader with responsibility for professional conduct and discipline, heads the Faculty of Advocates.

Approximately 460 members of the Faculty of Advocates are practising advocates. The remaining members include judges, sheriffs, academic and retired members.

For appearances in court, advocates are briefed by solicitors. The public cannot instruct advocates directly, although advocates can accept instructions directly from an individual or organisation in four main categories – legal professionals, other professionals, public authorities and a wide range of other individuals and bodies. Advocates also give their opinions on difficult or important legal problems referred to them by solicitors and, exceptionally, by others, and may supplement their practice by appearing before certain administrative tribunals and enquiries. Each advocate practises on his or her own; partnerships are not currently permitted. Practising advocates are either seniors or juniors. They enter as a junior and after ten to fifteen years' practice may apply through the Lord Justice General to be appointed Queen's Counsel by the Queen. This is known as 'taking silk' from the silk gowns worn by QCs in court. As a QC or senior, an advocate is entitled to be accompanied by a junior to assist him or her in the conduct of the case but may choose not to do so.

The Faculty of Advocates has its own professional examinations. However, prospective advocates usually obtain exemption from these by obtaining an appropriate law degree from a Scottish university and a postgraduate Diploma in Legal Practice. Prospective advocates must undergo a period of training in a solicitor's office, followed by training under a practising advocate (known as 'devilling', with the trainee advocate known as a 'devil'). During this period he or she undertakes an intensive advocacy skills course and must also take the Faculty of Advocates' examinations in certain practical subjects for which a law degree gives no exemption.

10.3.2 Solicitors

All practising solicitors must be members of the Law Society of Scotland, the statutory governing body of Scottish solicitors. Among other things, the society regulates admission to the solicitors' profession, represents solicitors in their relations with government, other bodies and the public; makes representations for law reform; enforces standards of professional conduct; and maintains a guarantee fund from which payments are made to people who have suffered pecuniary loss because of the dishonesty of a solicitor in practice (see 15.2.1).

Solicitors undertake most of the litigation in the sheriff courts. Most civil work concerns divorce and related family matters and actions for the recovery of debts. Criminal work covers a wide variety of cases. Many solicitors in private practice engage in 'chamber work' such as the buying and selling of domestic and commercial property, preparation of wills, estate management and management of trusts and executries.

The majority of solicitors are in private practice, that is, they practise alone or as partners in firms of solicitors, or as employed assistants to solicitors in private practice. An increasing number of solicitors are employed by local authorities, central government directorates (including procurators fiscal and officials of the Crown Office), by other public bodies and by industrial and commercial companies.

Like the Faculty of Advocates, the Law Society of Scotland has its own professional examinations, from which solicitors may obtain exemption by including the necessary professional subjects in a law degree of a Scottish university and completing a postgraduate Diploma in Legal Practice. A solicitor wishing to practise, whether on his or her own or in partnership or as an employed solicitor, must take out an annual practising certificate from the society, which keeps the Roll of Solicitors.

10.3.3 Solicitor advocates

While solicitors cannot appear before the superior courts, they can seek 'extended rights of audience', which allow them to represent clients as solicitor advocates in the Court of Session, the High Court of Justiciary, the House of Lords, the United Kingdom Supreme Court when it comes into being, and before the Judicial Committee of the Privy Council. Solicitors with at least five years' continuous experience of court work may apply to practise in the superior civil or criminal courts or both. They must undergo a training course in the work of the superior courts including observing cases in those courts, and pass examinations on practice, pleading and professional conduct in the superior courts, unless they have already passed the Faculty of Advocates' examinations. Solicitor advocates may also apply through the Lord Justice General to be appointed Queen's Counsel by the Queen.

10.4 Sheriff clerks and clerks to the district and justice of the peace courts

The sheriff clerk is the court official who is responsible for the throughput and administration of the court work in his or her sheriff court. The sheriff clerk or a member of his or her staff calls the cases in court, and sits in court during civil hearings and criminal trials and notes the outcome. Sheriff clerks and their staff are civil servants who are employed by the Scottish Court Service and are responsible for the day-to-day running of the sheriff court under the supervision of the sheriffs and the sheriff principal.

Clerks to the district court are members of the legal staff of the local authority. They are legally qualified and are responsible for the organisation of the court and the provision of legal advice to the bench.

Clerks to the justice of the peace court are members of the legal staff of the Scottish Court Service and play a similar role to clerks in the district courts.

10.5   Messengers-at-arms and sheriff officers

The courts or their officials do not carry out the functions of collecting sums due under decrees (court orders) of the Scottish courts, and of enforcing debts due under court decrees in the event of the debtor's failure to pay. After a decree is granted, the pursuer is left to recover the debt from the other person, and if unsuccessful must instruct a messenger-at-arms or sheriff officer to enforce the decree. The procedures for the enforcement of decrees are collectively known as diligence – see 5.6.

Messengers-at-arms enforce Court of Session decrees and sheriff officers enforce sheriff court decrees. In practice, however, many sheriff officers are also messengers-at-arms.

Messengers-at-arms are appointed and disciplined by the Lord Lyon King of Arms. Sheriff officers are appointed and disciplined by the appropriate sheriff principal. Messengers and sheriff officers charge fees that are prescribed by rules made by the Court of Session. Like solicitors, they may be in business on their own or in partnerships.

10.6   Fines enforcement officers

The Criminal Proceedings Etc. (Reform) (Scotland) Act 2007 provides for the introduction of fines enforcement officers. Fines enforcement officers, who are employed by the Scottish Court

Service, are responsible for the collection and enforcement of fines. They have at their disposal the power to ask the court to ensure the payment of fines by:

- making an order for deductions from benefits;

- making an order for deductions from earnings;

- making an order for arresting bank accounts;

- making an order for the seizure and sale of a motor vehicle belonging to the offender;

- sending the case back to court if none of these options work;

Fines enforcement officers will also provide help and advice to those who are having genuine difficulty in paying fines, and have the power to vary the instalment rate at which fines are to be paid.

11

The administration of the Scottish legal system

11.1 Introduction

The administration of the Scottish legal system has two main aspects: first, the organisation and administration of the courts and ancillary services; and second, the oversight and review of the law by Scottish Ministers and the promotion of law reform.

11.2 The organisation and administration of the courts

The administration of the supreme courts is the responsibility of the Lord President and the Lord Justice-General, who is the same person in his or her capacity as head of the civil and criminal courts respectively. In the case of the sheriff courts, this function is carried out by the sheriffs principal.

The supreme courts – the Court of Session and the High Court of Justiciary – enact the rules governing their own procedures and those of the sheriff and non-lawyer summary courts. The statutory Court of Session Rules Council and the Sheriff Court Rules Council, consisting of judges and legal practitioners (and in the case of the Sheriff Court Rules Council, two non-lawyers with a knowledge of civil court procedures and consumer affairs and an awareness of the interests of litigants), advise the supreme courts on amendments to the rules.

The First Minister is ultimately responsible for the central organisation and administration of the sheriff courts and, to a lesser extent, the supreme courts. He or she also decides on the number of sheriffs in each sheriffdom, and he or she may alter the boundaries of sheriffdoms and districts, create new ones and fix the places where the sheriff court is to be held. This responsibility is discharged by one of his or her ministers. The sheriff principal is responsible for the speedy and efficient conduct of business in his or her sheriffdom.

Sheriff courts have their own users' advisory committees who consider administrative matters to do with processing the business of that court, such as local court programming matters.

At the time of writing, the Scottish Parliament had approved the principles of the Judiciary and Courts (Scotland) Bill. The Bill establishes the Lord President as head of the Scottish judiciary with overall responsibility for the efficient disposal of business in all courts.

The Scottish Court Service is an executive agency of the Scottish Government Justice Directorate. It is responsible for the management and administration of Scotland's superior and sheriff courts. The Chief Executive of the Scottish Court Service is accountable to the Cabinet Secretary for Justice and through him or her to the Scottish Parliament for the administrative, organisational and technical services provided. The Judiciary and Courts (Scotland) Bill (see above) will introduce new governance arrangements for the Scottish Court Service, making it a non-ministerial department that will be run by a board with a judicial majority and chaired by the Lord President.

The Courts Group, which is also part of the Scottish Government Justice Directorate, is responsible, on behalf of the Lord Advocate, for the general oversight of certain parts of the legal system that are connected with the Scottish courts. These include, for example, the jurisdiction and procedure of the courts in civil proceedings, the rules for enforcement of court orders in civil proceedings, and policy functions such as reviewing the law of evidence, and civil jurisdiction in the courts.

The local authorities, advised by justices' committees, administer the district courts, providing them, for example, with buildings and clerks of court. The justices' committees approve the duty rota of justices and administer training schemes for justices set up by the First Minister. The Scottish Court Service administers justice of the peace courts (see 8.3).

The First Minister has overall responsibility for the Scottish legal system, although this is largely exercised by the Cabinet Secretary for Justice. His or her responsibilities include specific duties, for example, in relation to the appointment of judges. However, judges are not in any way subject to ministerial control and the independence of the courts is scrupulously observed.

Some of the functions of ministers are carried out by executive agencies, for example, the Registers of Scotland Executive Agency.

General responsibility is shared with the two law officers. The junior law officer is the Solicitor General for Scotland. He or she is a legal adviser to and member of the Scottish Government, and may appear for the Scottish Government in criminal or civil proceedings. The senior law officer is the Lord Advocate. He or she is a member of the Scottish Government, and is its chief legal adviser.

The Lord Advocate's department is responsible for drafting Scottish legislation. The Lord Advocate is responsible for prosecuting crime generally, through the Crown Office and the Crown Agent. In solemn criminal proceedings he or she is the named prosecutor (referred to as 'HM Advocate') and may appear himself or herself. In civil cases, the Lord Advocate sues on behalf of the Scottish Government and defends cases against it (referred to as 'Lord Advocate').

The Scotland Act 1998 created the post of Advocate General for Scotland, who is a minister of the United Kingdom government.

11.4   Agencies of law reform

The most important agency of law reform in Scotland is the Scottish Law Commission. The commission is a permanent statutory body of five members who have a duty to keep the whole of the law of Scotland under review with a view to its systematic development and reform. It has responsibilities for all areas of Scots law, including those reserved to the legislative competence of the United Kingdom Parliament. The commission is supported by a permanent staff. The Lord Advocate appoints the part-time chairman, who is a judge seconded from the Court of Session, and three full-time and one part-time commissioners. They are drawn from the judiciary, both branches of the legal profession and academic lawyers.

Law reform can be initiated by the commission itself or jointly with the Law Commission in England and Wales. Proposals can also come from organisations or individuals. Scottish Ministers may also ask the commission to undertake work on certain areas of the law. The commission's work is approved by Scottish Ministers or on the basis of a reference from Scottish Ministers. Proposals for law reform are made in the form of published reports, often with draft legislation attached, which are submitted to Scottish Ministers. In matters reserved to the United Kingdom Parliament, the report will also be submitted to the Secretary of State for Scotland.

Occasionally, review bodies or working parties are set up by ministers as temporary part-time bodies to make proposals for reform in particular areas of the law.

The Scottish Government and United Kingdom government departments may themselves publish tentative proposals or firm proposals for law reform in order to consult interested bodies before the introduction of legislation. The Scottish Government refers to tentative proposals as 'consultation documents' and firm proposals as 'consultation on draft legislation'. The United Kingdom Parliament refers to them as 'green papers' and 'white papers' respectively.

11.5 Other public offices

Apart from the directorates of the Scottish Government and departments of the United Kingdom government directly under ministerial control, a number of small autonomous public offices or departments, staffed by civil servants, provide essential services for the legal system. Some have been referred to elsewhere (see 4.6 and 9.3).

The Registers of Scotland Executive Agency maintains a number of public registers including the Land Register of Scotland, which was established under the Land Registration (Scotland) Act 1979 and records all interests in land. It is gradually replacing the General Register of Sasines, which is a register of title deeds relating to land transactions in Scotland.

The General Register Office for Scotland is a department of the Scottish Government responsible for the registration of births, deaths, marriages, civil partnerships, divorces, dissolution of civil partnerships and adoptions in Scotland, and for carrying out periodic censuses of Scotland's population. Other registries include the Register of Friendly Societies in Scotland, and the register of companies incorporated in Scotland under the Companies Act maintained by Companies House.

11.6 Further reading

Crown Office and Procurator Fiscal Service:
http://www.crownoffice.gov.uk

Scottish Government Justice Directorate:
http://www.scotland.gov.uk/Topics/Justice

The Scottish Court Service: a comprehensive guide. Available free from the Scottish Court Service, Hayweight House, 23 Lauriston Street, Edinburgh EH3 9DQ,
http://www.scotcourts.gov.uk

Judicial review

Judicial review of administrative action is a means of challenging in the courts the way in which decisions are reached by public authorities. Its purpose is to ensure that they act within the law. It is distinct from appeal, which challenges the merits of a decision.

All public authorities – government directorates, local authorities, statutory corporations, administrative tribunals, and the like – exist to perform functions defined and limited in varying degrees of detail by legislation or the rules of common law.

A public authority acts outwith the law (*ultra vires*) if it assumes a power that it does not by law possess, or if it uses its powers to defeat the objects for which the powers were conferred on it or for purposes that differ from those prescribed by law, or it fails to exercise its powers in accordance with the procedure laid down by law. Any person whose rights are injured, or threatened with injury, by an *ultra vires* or negligent act of a public authority, or by any failure of the authority to perform its statutory duties, may bring an action of judicial review to obtain the appropriate remedy.

Legal proceedings for judicial review can be raised only in the Court of Session. If the Court decides that the action or decision complained of is illegal, it can provide a number of different remedies, the more important of which are:

- Declarator: an order declaring the existence of a legal right.

- Interdict: an order that stops the public authority from doing something that is illegal. Interdict cannot be made against the Crown. The Court may grant interim interdict to maintain the *status quo* pending the Court's final decision.

- Reduction: an order that invalidates the decision complained of.

- Damages: an order awarding compensation for any damage caused by the negligent exercise of statutory powers or duties.

The characteristic flexibility of Scottish civil procedure enables all or any of these remedies to be obtained in one action.

The enactment of the Scotland Act 1998 and the Human Rights Act 1998 created new opportunities for judicial review. The availability of human rights directly enforceable before United Kingdom courts and the creation of the Scottish Parliament are likely to lead to the growth of judicial review and also to confirm its importance in the United Kingdom's constitution.

The Scotland Act provides for the United Kingdom or Scottish Law Officers to refer a Bill of the Scottish Parliament to the Judicial Committee of the Privy Council to settle a question of *vires*. A Bill may not be submitted for Royal Assent if it is the subject of a reference to the Judicial Committee. The Scotland Act also provides for dealing with the consequences of Acts of the Scottish Parliament or actions of the Scottish Government that are found to be outwith their powers.

For example, a Scottish Bill is outwith the competence of the parliament if it conflicts with the European Convention on Human Rights as incorporated in the Human Rights Act, and the Scotland Act prevents a member of the Scottish Government from making legislation if it is incompatible with the convention. The courts have powers to limit the retrospective effects of such Acts or actions. Provision is also made for the United Kingdom Parliament to make subordinate legislation to remedy the defect.

From October 2009, the jurisdiction of the Judicial Committee of the Privy Council over issues that raise questions about the actions of the Scottish Parliament or the Scottish Government will be assumed by the United Kingdom Supreme Court (see 4.4).

In certain activities of public authorities, for example, compulsory purchase of land, town and country planning, statutes provide for judicial review of whether the statutory procedures have been complied with.

13

Legal aid

13.1 Introduction

Legal aid is financial help from the state with legal costs. In Scotland, the Scottish Legal Aid Board administers legal aid.

Legal aid can be made available for civil and criminal actions and for general advice and assistance with legal problems. It is also available 'in respect of certain proceedings relating to children' (see 13.4) and for contempt of court proceedings.

There are strict financial limits on who qualifies for legal aid. Some people who qualify for civil legal aid have to make a financial contribution towards the grant of legal aid. Where a civil action for the recovery or preservation of money or other property succeeds, the Scottish Legal Aid Board is entitled to 'claw back' sufficient funds to meet any shortfall in respect of the legally-aided party's solicitor's fees, subject to regulations that provide for certain exclusions to this rule. Someone who is legally aided would not pay the expenses of his or her own solicitor if he or she lost the case but he or she may have to pay the legal expenses of the other side.

13.2 Advice and assistance

Advice and assistance is available to people with limited income and assets to obtain advice from a solicitor or, where appropriate, from an advocate, on any matter of Scots law. This includes, for example, questions relating to marriage, civil partnership and other matters affecting families and children (see 13.4), debt, employment, personal injury, landlord and tenant, neighbours, consumer law, wills, immigration, nationality and asylum. It does not usually cover representation in a court or tribunal, although a solicitor can give advice about and assistance with the preparation of a case or the negotiation of a settlement of a claim in such proceedings. However, there are exceptions for certain criminal proceedings (see 13.5.3).

13.2.1 *Assistance by way of representation in civil proceedings*

Assistance by way of representation, which is part of advice and assistance, allows representation to be provided for the following proceedings:

• Petitions for the appointment of an executor to a deceased person's estate.

• Civil proceedings arising from a failure by a person to pay a fine or other sum or obey an order of the court.

• Custody appearances under the Protection from Abuse and Matrimonial Homes Act.

It is also available in certain circumstances for proceedings before the following tribunals:

• The Mental Health Tribunal for Scotland.

• The Asylum and Immigration Tribunal.

• An employment tribunal.

• A VAT and duties tribunal.

13.3 Legal aid in civil proceedings

Legal aid may be available where a dispute or claim can only be settled by court action, or where someone is defending a civil case. For example, where someone has received advice and assistance on a legal matter and no resolution has been possible, he or she may be advised that the only course is to start a civil action. This type of legal aid covers proceedings in the sheriff court, the Court of Session, the House of Lords, the Lands Valuation Appeal Court, the Lands Tribunal for Scotland, the Scottish Land Court, the Employment Appeal Tribunal and the Judicial Committee of the Privy Council on appeal from the Court of Session, and will cover proceedings in the United

Kingdom Supreme Court (see 4.4) from October 2009. It is also available for proceedings before the Proscribed Organisations Appeals Commission and before the Social Security Commissioners and the Child Support Commissioners.

All types of action are included, except for election petitions, simplified actions of divorce, small claims at first instance and certain proceedings at first instance under the Debtors (Scotland) Act 1987. Also excluded are proceedings relating to the attachment of property under the Debt Arrangement and Attachment (Scotland) Act 2002. Legal aid or advice and assistance may also be available for mediation in some cases.

To be legally aided, an applicant must be financially eligible and the following conditions apply:

- legal aid is not available if someone else is prepared to assist or back the applicant, such as a trade union or insurance company;
- there must be sound grounds for taking, defending or being party to the proceedings;
- legal aid is not available if it is unreasonable in the circumstances to grant it – for instance, it would be unreasonable to grant legal aid to take a minor action in a superior court if a less expensive action in the sheriff court would be sufficient.

Where legal aid is refused on the merits of the case, the decision can be reviewed.

13.4 Legal aid in proceedings involving children

Advice and assistance is available for people who have to attend a children's hearing. That could include advice to the child if he or she is old enough to understand and directly instruct a solicitor to act for him or her, and advice to the child's parents or carers. It will not, however, cover a solicitor appearing at a children's hearing or in court.

Legal aid may provide funding for a solicitor and, where appropriate counsel, to take a case to court, for instance in a case that has been referred from a children's hearing to the sheriff court or where the parent, carer or child wishes to appeal a decision of a children's hearing or to appeal to a sheriff principal or even to the Court of Session, the decision that a sheriff has reached in a sheriff court. Children's legal aid is not, however, available for a solicitor to attend a children's hearing even where the related court proceedings are ongoing.

13.5 Legal aid in criminal proceedings

Criminal legal aid is available to the accused person in prosecutions brought in the district and justice of the peace courts, the sheriff court, the High Court and in appeals from all criminal courts.

In solemn proceedings, the court decides whether to grant legal aid. It is also for the court to decide whether to grant legal aid where a person who has not previously been sentenced to imprisonment or detention has been convicted in summary proceedings and the court is considering such a sentence. In summary cases, legal assistance may be available either by application to the board or by assistance by way of representation (see 13.5.3).

13.5.1 Accused person in custody

An accused person who is taken into custody, even if released on bail, will usually have a right to automatic free legal aid from the duty solicitor up to and including the first court appearance. A duty solicitor is available at every district, justice of the peace and sheriff court to advise accused persons in custody. The duty solicitor can also represent someone appearing in an identification parade.

Anyone who wants criminal legal aid for a case in the district or justice of the peace court, the sheriff court, the High Court of Justiciary or the Court of Criminal Appeal can choose between a private solicitor or a public defence solicitor employed by the Public Defence Solicitors' Office, which is directly funded by the Scottish Legal Aid Board. The Public Defence Solicitors'

Office has offices in Glasgow, Edinburgh, Inverness, Ayr, Dundee, Falkirk and Kirkwall.

13.5.2 Accused person not in custody

Advice and assistance may be available to someone who has been served with a summary complaint, depending on his or her financial circumstances. Where an accused person intends to plead not guilty, an application for criminal legal aid can only be made after that plea to the court.

13.5.3 Assistance by way of representation

Assistance by way of representation allows a solicitor, in certain circumstances, to represent a client who is not in custody and who intends to plead guilty or wishes to have his or her case continued or has changed his or her plea to guilty, provided no application for legal aid has been made.

13.5.4 Appeal against conviction or sentence

Someone convicted in a criminal court can get advice on a question of appeal, using advice and assistance or under any existing legal aid cover for the initial proceedings. In a case where leave to appeal is needed and this is granted, the financial test is applied if it is needed. In other cases, legal aid will be granted where the board decides that it is in the interests of justice to make legal aid available to the applicant, and the financial tests are met.

13.6 Further reading

Scottish Legal Aid Board, guidance leaflets on legal aid in Scotland. Available free from the Scottish Legal Aid Board, 44 Drumsheugh Gardens, Edinburgh EH3 7SW, http://www.slab.org.uk

Other sources of assistance

14.1 Citizens advice bureaux

Citizens advice bureaux form a network that covers Scotland. Most are organised by full-time managers and staffed by trained unpaid volunteers. The government funds the central support organisation, Citizens Advice Scotland, which provides training and a comprehensive information system, and sets standards for local bureaux. The local authorities provide local funding.

Citizens advice bureaux provide basic advice and assistance on legal problems with the support of Citizens Advice Scotland. Where legal services are required, bureaux can refer people to local solicitors or to legal clinics provided by local solicitors, often utilising the legal aid advice and assistance scheme (see 13.2).

14.2 Money advice services

Money advice services are specialised agencies set up to assist with debt problems arising from credit, mortgages and loans, etc. They are provided by citizens advice bureaux, local authority consumer and trading standards departments and independent advice agencies. They act as intermediaries for people with multiple debt problems by negotiating repayments on their behalf, so reducing the incidence of debt enforcement and bankruptcy. Money Advice Scotland supports some of the agencies and provides training and a forum for the exchange of views.

14.3 Law centres

Law centres are non-profit making charitable bodies staffed by solicitors and support staff. They provide legal services in deprived areas not otherwise provided by traditional legal services, and specialise in areas such as social security, housing, consumer issues, asylum and immigration. They also provide training for local organisations and raise awareness of the law and legal issues. Law centres in Scotland are concentrated in urban areas.

14.4 In-court advice

In-court advice services funded by the Scottish Government are located in the sheriff courts in Aberdeen, Airdrie, Dundee, Edinburgh, Hamilton and Kilmarnock. They are run by a variety of organisations: local citizens advice bureaux manage the services in Aberdeen, Airdrie, Hamilton and Edinburgh; the service in Dundee is jointly managed by the local citizens advice bureau and Shelter; and East Ayrshire Council manages the service in Kilmarnock. They are intended to extend access to civil justice to people without legal representation in certain legal proceedings, primarily small claims cases, summary cause cases, heritable (housing) and debt cases. The Scottish Government also funds a homelessness advice service at Paisley Sheriff Court and the Legal Services Agency provides a defended eviction service in Glasgow and Greenock sheriff courts.

14.5 Qualified conveyancers and executry practitioners

The Law Reform (Miscellaneous Provisions) (Scotland) Act 1990 provided for non-solicitors to become qualified conveyancers and executry practitioners and offer services to the public for a fee. In 2003, responsibility for their regulation was transferred to the Law Society of Scotland. After the transfer, no new independent conveyancers and executry practitioners were allowed to register, although those already registered were able to continue practising. Most qualified conveyancers and executry practitioners are employed by solicitors.

14.6 Trades unions

Some of the larger trades unions provide legal services for their members. These may be provided by their own staff or through firms of solicitors, and may include advice on any legal problem and, if there is a case to be pursued, how it may be financed, for example, by the union.

14.7 Insurance companies

Some insurance companies offer their policyholders optional cover for personal legal advice and expenses, which is also know as legal expenses insurance, and is usually offered as an 'add on' to household or motor insurance policies. It may cover the costs of legal advice and the costs of pursuing or defending legal actions relating to, for example, consumer disputes, claims for death or injury, claims connected with their homes, neighbour disputes, the recovery of insured losses from a motor accident and claims connected with a contract of employment.

14.8 Claims management services

There are companies and individuals that offer claims management services in relation to claims for compensation. In Scotland, these are primarily in relation to claims for compensation for personal injury. While the Compensation Act 2006 regulates services in England and Wales, those in Scotland are not regulated.

14.9 Will writers

There are individuals and companies, which may be based outwith Scotland, which offer will-writing services. Some are members of a professional association, but the law does not regulate them.

Protection of the public

15.1 Introduction

The legal profession is largely self-regulating. However, there are a number of protections for solicitors' clients and rather fewer for clients of advocates. Solicitors' and advocates' professional bodies have their own internal complaints and disciplinary procedures, overseen by the Scottish Legal Services Ombudsman (see 15.6). From 1 October 2008 the Scottish Legal Complaints Commission (see 15.7) will replace the ombudsman as the gateway for all complaints. The commission will retain, deal with and determine service complaints and pass conduct matters to the relevant legal professional bodies. Therefore, the procedures described in 15.2 (except for the references to the Scottish Solicitor's Guarantee fund) and 15.3 will change when the commission is in operation.

15.2 Solicitors

Solicitors must be covered by insurance against claims for damages (see 15.2.2), and they must contribute to the Scottish Solicitor's Guarantee Fund, which is maintained by the Law Society of Scotland to provide protection for clients of dishonest solicitors. The Law Society of Scotland also has powers to deal with complaints about solicitors' professional misconduct, and, until the Scottish Legal Complaints Commission (see 15.7) commences, with claims of inadequate professional services. Auditors of Court have powers to reduce excessive fees.

15.2.1 Dishonesty

Compensation from the guarantee fund may be paid to people who have suffered loss because of the dishonesty of solicitors. The fund is a last resort after other remedies such as civil recovery through the court have been pursued and have failed. Solicitors make an annual contribution to the fund, and may be required to make additional payments to meet exceptional demands.

15.2.2 Professional negligence

A solicitor who does not exercise a reasonable standard of care and skill may be sued for consequential loss by a client, and possibly by third parties, on the grounds of negligence. Negligence may include failure to register documents and failing to start actions within the required time limits. The Law Society of Scotland requires all its members to be covered by its master policy of professional indemnity insurance.

15.2.3 Inadequate professional services and excessive fees

Inadequate professional services are those that fall short of negligence. Currently, the Law Society of Scotland has powers, on making a finding of inadequate professional service, to order a reduction or waiver of fees, a refund, a rectification of errors and omissions, and payment to the complainer of up to £5,000 as compensation for inconvenience in relation to business on-going or commenced after 1 April 2005, or £1000 for business before that. When the Scottish Legal Complaints Commission (see 15.7) commences, it will have substantially greater powers.

If the Council of the Society decides after proper enquiry that the fees charged by a solicitor are grossly excessive, it has the power to suspend the solicitor from practice until the Auditor of Court has taxed the fees, and the solicitor has paid any refund due to the client. This power is very rarely exercised, as solicitors will almost always have the account taxed voluntarily.

15.2.4 Discipline

Where the Council of the Law Society believes that a solicitor may be guilty of professional misconduct, the matter may be referred for prosecution before the independent Scottish Solicitors Discipline Tribunal.

Under the Legal Profession and Legal Aid (Scotland) Act 2007, the Scottish Solicitors Discipline Tribunal comprises two pools – one of solicitor members and one of non-solicitor members who are appointed by the Lord President of the Court of Session. The tribunal will normally sit with six members – three solicitors and three non-solicitors.

Where a solicitor has been convicted of an offence involving dishonesty or has been sentenced to imprisonment of over two years, the society is required to report the matter to the tribunal for consideration. If a solicitor is convicted of some other offence and sentenced to less than two years' imprisonment the society is required to consider whether the matter should be prosecuted formally before the tribunal as professional misconduct.

The tribunal also currently considers appeals by solicitors against determinations of inadequate professional service by the society. Once the Legal Profession and Legal Aid (Scotland) Act has been fully enacted the tribunal will also have jurisdiction to consider appeals made by complainers or solicitors in relation to matters of unsatisfactory professional conduct. The tribunal's role in considering inadequate professional service appeals will diminish following the introduction of the Scottish Legal Complaints Commission (see 15.7) to deal directly with service complaints.

The tribunal has the power to strike off, suspend from practice, censure and fine a solicitor up to £10,000, and to restrict a solicitor in relation to practice, for example, to practising only as an assistant with a firm. The tribunal also has powers similar to those of the society when considering appeals against decisions of inadequate professional service. Its decisions are published, unless to do so would harm persons other than the solicitor, partners and their families or prejudice any future criminal prosecution.

15.3 Advocates

Advocates, like other lawyers, may be held liable for negligent advice unconnected with court proceedings. Apart from that, the law is currently uncertain. The House of Lords has ruled on two occasions that, on public interest grounds, it was inappropriate for lawyers engaged in litigation to be subject to negligence claims. Although a different view was taken in an English case in 2000, certain of the grounds relied on would not apply in Scotland, and their Lordships expressly confirmed that the position in Scotland was not under consideration in that appeal.

15.3.1 Discipline

Anyone can complain about the behaviour of an advocate to the Dean of the Faculty of Advocates. The Dean will refer complaints in the first instance to a complaints committee, which includes equal advocate and non-lawyer representation. If the committee upholds all or part of the complaint it can impose verbal admonition, a formal written reprimand, a severe written censure, an order for cancellation or total or partial repayment of any fees charged for the work which led to the complaint or a fine of up to £7,500. As well as a fine, it can suspend an advocate from practice for up to a year. The complaints committee may also remit the matter to an investigating committee if material facts are in dispute or to the Disciplinary Tribunal, which is chaired by a retired Senator of the College of Justice or a sheriff principal and has a formal procedure. The tribunal can impose a fine of up to £15,000, and may order suspension or expulsion of the advocate concerned. Decisions of the tribunal may be subject to judicial review in the Court of Session (see Chapter 12).

15.4 Judges

15.4.1 Introduction

Someone who is dissatisfied with the outcome of a case, and who thinks that the judge or sheriff was wrong, can only appeal their decision to a higher court, if a right of appeal exists in the particular circumstances.

15.4.2 Superior court judges

The First Minister, on the recommendation of the Scottish Parliament, may remove a superior court judge from office 'by reason of inability, neglect of duty, or misbehaviour'. If such a decision is under consideration, an investigating tribunal must be formed which reports its findings to the Scottish Parliament.

The Judiciary and Courts (Scotland) Bill, which was before the Scottish Parliament at the time of writing, provides for the First Minister to set up such a tribunal when requested to do so by the Lord President or in other such circumstances as he thinks fit.

15.4.3 Sheriffs

The First Minister can also remove a sheriff from office. If, after investigation by the Lord President and the Lord Justice-Clerk, a sheriff is reported as not fit for office 'by reason of inability, neglect of duty, or misbehaviour' the First Minister may make a statutory instrument (subject to annulment by the Scottish Parliament) removing him or her. This happens very rarely.

Part-time sheriffs can be removed from office only by order of a tribunal of three members appointed by the Lord President of the Court of Session.

The Judiciary and Courts (Scotland) Bill, which was before the Scottish Parliament at the time of writing, provides for the First Minister to set up such a tribunal to investigate and report on whether a person is unfit to hold judicial office when requested to do so by the Lord President or in other such circumstances as he or she thinks fit. Sheriffs principal, sheriffs and part-time sheriffs will all be subject to the jurisdiction of such a tribunal.

15.4.4 Justices of the peace

A full justice in a district court may be removed from office or be restricted to having the functions of a signing justice (see 10.1.3) only by order of a tribunal of three members appointed by the Lord President of the Court of Session.

A justice in a justice of the peace court may be removed from office by order of a tribunal instigated by the sheriff principal of the sheriffdom to which the justice is appointed on the recommendation of a Justices' Appraisal Committee.

The Scottish Court Service has a procedure for considering complaints about any of its services. These include the services provided by any members of the Principal Clerk's staff (in the supreme courts) or the Regional Sheriff Clerk's staff (in the sheriff courts).

15.6 The Scottish Legal Services Ombudsman

The ombudsman is an independent non-lawyer investigator, appointed by Scottish Ministers. He or she currently investigates and reports on complaints made against legal services professional organisations about the way they have dealt with a complaint against a practitioner. The professional organisations are the Law Society of Scotland and the Faculty of Advocates. The Scottish Legal Complaints Commission is due to replace the ombudsman on 1 October 2008 – see 15.7.

Any person who has a complaint against a legal practitioner that has been investigated by one of the professional bodies or one that the professional body has declined to investigate may complain to the ombudsman. Complaints to the ombudsman about unsatisfactory handling of a complaint by a professional body must be made within six months of the body's decision.

The ombudsman cannot over-rule the decisions of the professional body. He or she can only recommend a particular form of redress or further investigation on a particular complaint, or make general recommendations on dealing with complaints to the professional body or, where necessary, to Scottish Ministers. He or she may also take a case of potential professional misconduct direct to the Scottish Solicitors Discipline Tribunal.

15.7 Scottish Legal Complaints Commission

The Scottish Legal Complaints Commission, which was created by the Legal Profession and Legal Aid (Scotland) Act 2007, is scheduled to open on 1 October 2008. The commission, which will operate independently of the legal professional bodies, will receive all complaints about legal practitioners (that is, solicitors who are members of the Law Society of Scotland, advocates who are members of the Faculty of Advocates, conveyancing or executry practitioners regulated by the Law Society of Scotland, or any other body or person as further defined by section 46 of the Legal Profession and Legal Aid (Scotland) Act 2007) and decide whether the complaint is about service or conduct. It will deal with complaints about service and refer complaints about conduct to the relevant professional organisation. However, it will have an oversight role in relation to how the professional body investigates conduct complaints.

The commission will have the power to mediate, resolve or determine a service complaint, and will also have the power to declare the complaint premature if the complainer has not attempted to resolve it directly with the firm.

The Commission will only deal with complaints relating to work carried out by a legal practitioner on or after 1 October 2008; the existing professional bodies will deal with complaints about work before that date. New compensation levels will apply to service complaints that are upheld. The commission will have the power to award compensation up to a maximum amount of £20,000 to a client in respect of a service complaint. Where the complaint has been referred to the relevant professional body as an alleged issue of unsatisfactory professional conduct, a maximum amount of £5,000 will be payable.

15.8   Further reading

Law Society of Scotland/Scottish Consumer Council, *Getting the best from your solicitor*. Law Society of Scotland, Edinburgh, 2004. Available free from The Law Society of Scotland, 26 Drumsheugh Gardens, Edinburgh EH3 7YR: http://www.lawscot.org.uk/

Scottish Legal Complaints Commission: http://www.scottishlegalcomplaints.com

Scottish Legal Services Ombudsman, *Annual Report*. The Stationery Office, Edinburgh. The current report can also be found at http://www.slso.org.uk/reports.shtml

Index

Note: **bold** page numbers indicate chapters. *Italics* indicate dates.

see also civil courts
civil partnership, end of 31, 39
civil procedure 18-19, **27-37**
  appeals 35-6
  diligence 34-5
  fatal accident and sudden death
    enquiries 36-7
  legal aid in 78-9
  remedies 34
  representation in 78-9
  special courts and tribunals 33
  see also civil law; Court of
    Session; Sheriff Court
claims management services 84
clerks of court 67-8
  Lord Justice-Clerk 22, 47, 61,
    89
College of Justice 2, 88
Committee of Permanent
Representatives (COREPER)
  9
common law 1-2, 3, 6, 12-13, 17,
  20-1
Commonwealth jurisdiction 24
community-service orders 58
Companies Act (1985) 21, 74
compensation
  Acts (1995 and 2006) 59-60, 84
  order 58
  for solicitor's dishonesty 85-6
Complaints Commission 85, 86,
  87, 90-1
consistorial remedies 34
consultation documents 73
`consumer contracts' 21
Consumer Credit Act (2006) 33
Consumer Focus Scotland x
contract
  `consumer' 21
  law of 16
conveyancing practitioners 83

conviction, appeal against 81
COREPER (Committee of
Permanent Representatives) 9
Council of Europe 10, 12
Council of Ministers of
European Union 8, 9, 13
Court of Criminal Appeal 5, 46,
  59, 80
Court of Exchequer in Scotland
  25
Court of First Instance 9-10, 24
Court of Justice, European 9-10,
  23, 24, 28, 46, 65
Court of Session 2, 4-5, 18, 24,
  25, 70
  actions in 28-9
  administration 46
  advocates in 65
  children's hearings 43, 80
  decree 35
  fees rules created by 68
  Inner House 4, 22-3
  judicial review 75-6
  legal aid 78
  Outer House 4, 22
  petitions in 29-30
  Rules Council 70
  solicitor advocates 62, 67
  tribunals 42, 43
  universal civil jurisdiction 4-5
  see also Lord President
courts
  levels of see inferior courts;
    superior courts organisation
    and administration
    of 70-1, 90
  see also civil courts; Court of
    Justice; Court of Session;
    criminal courts; Sheriff
    Court; special jurisdiction
Courts Group 71

administration 46
appeals to 58-9
Lord Justice-Clerk 22, 47, 61, 89
Lord Justice-General 47, 62, 65, 70
legal aid in 80
nobile officium 30, 34, 48
referral to 56
solicitor advocates in 62, 67
witness support 57
`HM Advocate' *see* Lord Advocate
HM Revenue and Customs 41, 49
House of Lords 4, 18, 28
  Appellate Committee of 23-4
  and judges, appointment of 61
  legal aid 78
  solicitor advocates in 65, 67
  on solicitor negligence 87-8
Housing (Scotland) Act 2006 12-13
Human Rights Act (*1998*) 11-12, 50, 76
Human Rights, European Court of 11, 12, 65
Hume, David 3

imprisonment 57
inadequate professional services from solicitors 86, 87-8
in-court advice 83
Independent Consumer Arbitration Service 39
`indictment' 17
inferior courts 18
  see also district; justices of the peace; sheriff court
inhibition of sale 35
injury offences 17
Inner House of Court of Session 4, 22-3

Inspector of Taxes 42
insurance companies, assistance from 84
interdict order 34, 75
intermediate diet in summary criminal procedure 53-4
international private law 16-17

Jones, T H 60
judges 61-4
  appointment of 61
  public protection from 88-9
  sheriff 63, 89-90
  in superior courts 61-2, 88-9
  temporary 62
  trial without jury 17
  see also justices of the peace
Judicial Appointments Board for Scotland 62, 63
Judicial Committee of Privy Council 24, 65, 67, 76, 78
judicial procedure *see* civil procedure; criminal procedure
judicial system **18-19**
  see also civil courts
Judiciary and Courts (Scotland) Bill 71, 89
juries/jurors 3
  civil cases 29
  criminal cases 56
  solemn procedure 56-7
  trial without 17
Justice, European Court of 9-10, 23, 24, 28, 46, 65
Justice-Clerk, Lord 22, 47, 61, 89
Justice-General of High Court of Justiciary, Lord 47, 62, 65, 70
Justices' Appraisal Committee 89
justices of the peace 18, 46, 71, 89
  clerks to court 68